PRAISE FOR *TRANSFORMII*

"When transitions are challenging, the trick is to find simplicity on the other side of the complexity. *Transforming Sales Management* offers useful guidance for navigating change but does so in the form of six easy-to-remember yet potentially penetrating questions that can be used to forge a path forward."
Daryl Conner, global change leader, Chairman of Conner Advisory and Conner Academy, author of *Managing at the Speed of Change* (1993) and *Leading at the Edge of Chaos* (1998)

"This book, the model and the tools that underlie it should be well-thumbed, bookmarked and used by sales managers who need to help their teams get over their fears, their limiting beliefs and tendencies to procrastinate so they can increase sales. It is also my firm belief that the book should be in the knapsack of every sales leader, manager, coach and trainer."
Dr. David Wilkinson, Editor-in-Chief of *The Oxford Review*, author of *The Ambiguity Advantage*

"Change is scary! People tend to be resistant to change (whether positive or negative), which is why successful organizational transformations are so notoriously difficult to achieve. Grant Van Ulbrich's refreshing new book *Transforming Sales Management* factors in individual choice and provides guidance for people in business and beyond on how to manage their own change situation. Taking his original research (first published in the *International Journal of Sales Transformation*), Dr. Van Ulbrich outlines his 'SCARED SO WHAT' personal-change model. The book can help salespeople globally navigate their own personal change journey (at work or even in their personal lives). Importantly, the book explores real-world examples and applications of the model from within the hospitality industry, most notably during a period of unprecedented societal and business

transformation triggered by the global Covid pandemic. Accessible and easy to read, this book offers a ground-breaking but practical guide to understanding the role of individuals' emotions in executing business change."
Nick de Cent, Editor-in-Chief of *The International Journal of Sales Transformation*

"As a scholar practitioner and learning leader in organizations, Grant's pragmatic review of popular change models reminded me of 'the basics' but his work provided a fresh perspective about the human emotions that too often go overlooked when preparing for and leading through change events—and not just for sales organizations, but all organizations! I reviewed each component of SCARED SO WHAT and re-thought certain elements of the change happening around me and put forth my own personal change strategy plan in a straightforward way using Grant's model."
Mark C. Boccia, Chief Learning Officer at Amazon

"Grant has written a modern, must-read book about the ongoing challenges of change and transformation, not just for millennials, but for all of us facing the increasing pace of the VUCA world in which we all live. What makes his book so notable is that it doesn't just explain a theory, but also considers practice and tools."
Waldemar Adams, Senior Vice President Market Advisory of SAP Customer Success

"Change is constant—in our personal lives and professional careers. Navigating change effectively allows people to learn from change and move forward in a positive way. Dr Grant Van Ulbrich's new book, *Transforming Sales Management* presents an opportunity to learn the how and why our reactions to change can affect outcomes. Grant takes the reader through established models and shares his own model: SCARED SO WHAT. Whether reading from a managerial or organizational perspective, or as an individual, this book will provide you with an actionable process for making the most of your experiences with change."
Marty Holmes, Executive Director of Sales Education Foundation (SEF)

"*Transforming Sales Management* is a must-read for all leaders as it goes beyond just sales. It's a book that is easy to enjoy and follow because it does not just describe theories. Rather, it uses real-world scenarios and provides personal and practical examples to follow. In my own reflection after reading this book, it is our people that are at the centre of any transformation. How we support them means we must include them in on the journey. This book provides the new tools to show us all how."

Olga C. Piqueras, Managing Director of Port Operations for Intercruises Shoreside & Port Services

"Organizations don't change; people within organizations change. Grant takes a much-needed look at the individual as the linchpin of transformation efforts and presents a model of individual change that will help you understand how to navigate change in your own life and how to work with others who are trying to navigate their own changes."

Dr. Willy Bolander, Professor of Industrial Distribution and Associate Director of the Read Center for Distribution at Texas A&M University

"I love the model as it really does drill down and make you think out of the box and will help professionals not only in their work but also their personal life as well."

Mark Robinson, Senior Vice President Operations of Scenic Luxury Cruises & Tours

"A progressive and empowering approach for aiding individual stakeholders in making their personal decisions about accepting change."

Theresa Moulton, Chief Editor of *The Change Management Review*

"The journey this book supports is one that many sales leaders fail to recognize as fundamentally important. The most vital asset to any company is its salespeople. Not the technology they use, nor the products they sell, but the people they forge relations with, and how they do so in an ever-changing world. Salespeople need to transform constantly, to remain the competitive advantage for themselves and their companies. I challenge the reader not to keep returning to this guide on personal change. Comprehensive references call for the curious to continue to develop knowledge on change and keep learning. Grant expertly points out that change is a 'messy process' and this book lifts the 'learning fog' that envelopes us when trying to change ourselves."

Andrew Hough, Founder Institute of Sales Professionals and Sales Researcher Cranfield University

Transforming Sales Management

Lead Sales Teams Through Change

Grant Van Ulbrich

KoganPage

First published in Great Britain and the United States in 2023 by Kogan Page Limited

2nd Floor, 45 Gee Street
London
EC1V 3RS
United Kingdom

8 W 38th Street, Suite 902
New York, NY 10018
USA

4737/23 Ansari Road
Daryaganj
New Delhi 110002
India

www.koganpage.com

© SCARED SO WHAT Ltd 2023

ISBNs

Hardback   978 1 3986 0910 5
Paperback   978 1 3986 0908 2
Ebook   978 1 3986 0909 9

British Library Cataloguing-in-Publication Data

A CIP record for this book is available from the British Library.

Library of Congress Control Number

2023933904

Typeset by Integra Software Services, Pondicherry
Print production managed by Jellyfish
Printed and bound by CPI Group (UK) Ltd, Croydon, CR0 4YY

I dedicate this book to my mom, Brenda, and dad, Ernie, for their never-ending support throughout my life in saying that I can do whatever I set in my mind to achieve. To my brother Jaime, for always being the first to lead and leading with such grace, pride, and professionalism. To my best friend, partner, and spouse Claudio, I say thank you so much for never doubting my abilities and always encouraging me to keep going even when I thought I could not. You've all been my champions and my family.

CONTENTS

LIST OF FIGURES AND TABLES

ABOUT THE AUTHOR

Dr. Grant Van Ulbrich is Global Director of Sales Transformation at Royal Caribbean Group. He leads the industry as the first person to graduate with distinction with a Master of Science in Professional Practice in Leading Sales Transformation from Middlesex University and the Consalia Sales Business School. He is also the first person in the cruise and hospitality industry to graduate with a Doctorate of Professional Studies with a concentration in Leading Sales Transformation, with Middlesex University as well.

He is Founding Fellow of the Institute of Sales Professionals and is a certified sales transformation coach with Consalia Sales Business School and the Institute of Leadership and Management.

Grant's personal change model—SCARED SO WHAT™—is used by Royal Caribbean International's sales teams worldwide, and it is used by B2B travel industry customers. His work on it has been published and publicly reviewed in *The International Journal of Sales Transformation*, *The Change Management Review*, and *The Oxford Review*. He has led presentations for the change management model countless times for Royal Caribbean and recently at the Sales Educators' Academy Conference, the Institute of Sales Professionals, and the former Association of Professional Sales.

Hailing from the US state of Kansas, Grant currently lives together with his spouse in London, England. Together they enjoy the local theatre, music, and culture of living in Europe. His passion is in supporting the professionalization of the sales career pathway, coaching and investing in sales team members, and speaking on behalf of the global sales community in living through the Consalia sales mindsets and championing an individual's own ability to manage personal change.

FOREWORD

It was October 2018 when I first met Grant in person. He was very uncertain then about his ability to complete the Master's program he had just embarked on—Leading Sales Transformation. Who would have thought then that he would have a book, *Transforming Sales Management: Lead Sales Teams Through Change*, published? Not me and probably not Grant. So, what led to this?

I remember Grant looking rather upset with his arms crossed during the "Leading Collaborative Change" module of the master's program. He had just been taken through a number of organizational change models, so I asked him what was wrong. He said that they just did not work for him. I remember asking myself at this point: Did Grant not understand these models? Was he being rather arrogant, challenging the great change gurus? I responded, "Well then, why don't you, for your next assessed project, create your own change model and see if it works?" He did just that.

So, he went studying change models in detail and figuring out which model is fit for which purpose—not only content to read up about change these models but also in some cases to talk directly to the creators.

What makes Grant qualified to write this book about change? As readers, we need to know he has conducted due diligence on its content and even better if it's written with authenticity. We are engaged if the author is not just hypothetically writing about transformation, but Grant has really "lived" it, has deeply experienced change not just at an organizational level but also at a personal level.

There can't be that many sectors that were so dramatically affected by the pandemic as the leisure industry and within that industry the cruise segment was arguably the most impacted. Grant in his role as Director of Sales Transformation was uniquely positioned to witness change at multiple levels across the many different functions of the business.

It's clear from the outset, through the tone and style of this book, that he brilliantly connects his research on the academic theoretical change frameworks with his personal journey of change. He has put himself at the center of his enquiry into change. In doing so, he fully justifies the reason why established organizational change models did not do it for him. As he says, "I found that the other models were useful and valid but were designed for organizational use rather than personal and individual use." The SARA Curve, adapted from Kübler-Ross' 5 Stages of Grief®, is often (wrongly, as Grant explains) referred to the go-to process for managing change in business settings for organizational change—he argues that it was never intended for that purpose. So, this journey is why he created the SCARED SO WHAT model—a model designed to help people manage personal change.

The early chapters in the book are an incredibly useful reference for eight key change models—these include Kotter, Lewin, Hiatt, McKinsey, Kübler-Ross, SARA, and Conner's positive and negative response curves. It's clear the energy from Grant's book comes from Chapter 4 onwards, where he describes the reason why personal change models are essential to navigate the choppy seas of transformation and then goes on to share his research and the frameworks for dealing with change at a personal level.

What we have here is one reference book that enables the reader with information that can equip them with change and transformation models at both an organizational and personal level from which the model, most appropriate, can be selected.

We live in times of fast change at multiple levels—health pandemics, war, nationalism, supply chain disruption, interest rate variations, recession, technical/digital disruption, and political situations. Our ability to be agile, to take control of the change process, to seek opportunities within such a change context to develop personally and organizationally, is surely one of the key competencies of this modern era in which we live. Therefore, this book is incredibly relevant now. The fact that Grant has also included many practical examples makes this a book that is not just helpful in knowing what to do, but how to do change.

So, on a personal note, thank you Grant for helping us have a better grasp of what it takes to manage change. Thanks also for creating a new model—SCARED SO WHAT—to help us manage change at a personal level and for reminding us that we can take control with the tools to do so. You are a brilliant role model for future thought leaders who are being empowered through their Master's degrees and even beyond.

Dr. Philip Squire

CEO, The Consalia Sales Business School

Author of *Selling Transformed: Develop the Sales Values which Deliver Competitive Advantage*

www.Consalia.com

ACKNOWLEDGMENTS

It is very important that I take time to acknowledge a few distinguished members that for without their guidance and support of me and my career, none of what is in this book would have come to fruition.

First and foremost, to Mr. Stuart Leven. I thank you so much for believing in my ability to do more and be more. It is because of you and your guidance and encouragement that in my mid-40s I would begin university to participate in the world's first Master of Science program to lead sales transformation. Not only did you champion me to enrol, but you stood by me and coached me throughout the program as I applied my learnings to the business. Thank you so much for your never-ending belief in developing people. You are a true champion of others.

Brian Tilley is in a league of his own. I had never had an executive coach, but I am so honored to have had the opportunity to have one and blessed to have been assigned to you. You have become more than a leadership coach; you have become a lifelong mentor and friend. You pulled me out of the 100-page PowerPoint decks and transformed me into someone with a bit more clarity and focus. Now I put it all into this book... and think of you. Thanks so very much for developing and encouraging me to keep growing.

Dr. Phillip Squire, you are in a league of your own. As the founder of the Consalia Sales Business School, I cannot thank you enough for being my professor and guru on this sales transformation journey. Thank you for pioneering the sales master's programs in science and psychology. And thank you for not allowing me to just use the current models for change but encouraging me to be bold and daring to create my own. This book is because of your belief in me. More than a professor, you too are a lifelong friend. Thank you for being the sales education pioneer.

Sean Treacy is a gentleman of the highest calibre. Not only was I blessed to have Stuart as an investor in people for a supervisor, but I was also continually blessed to transition under your leadership where the same belief was held. You too are a champion of professional development and supporting the growth of others. Thank you for believing in the research and allowing SCARED SO WHAT to go out to all our employees and our travel customers in our international remit.

To Josue Santiago, an executive change management practitioner and guru, I say thank you. You took full support of SCARED SO WHAT for our people and helped me make the SCARED quiz a simple, helpful, and easy tool to use by others in navigating change. I truly applaud your leadership and thank you so much for your friendship and guidance.

And to all of the employees and travel customers throughout the world that participated in using SCARED SO WHAT within our sales environment and during the pandemic. Using the model for yourselves and your families provided the research data to allow me to continue building and developing the model in my goal to help not only you, but countless others. Thank you.

Introduction

*Sales transformation, sales management,
and change management, and the importance
of learning how to manage personal change*

The very fact that you have chosen to take on this book shows that you are curious about transforming your sales management practice or yourself. You are a seeker of knowledge, and a person who would like not only to invest in yourself but also for those who are in your care. And for that, I am grateful you made this decision. Continuing to develop your skillsets and competencies by gaining knowledge provides you with invaluable insight to share not only with others but for yourself and your sales practice. *Transforming Sales Management* is 100 percent about accepting and leading change by learning how to manage it for yourself—perhaps for the first time.

Although I have enjoyed well over 25 years of global retail and commercial sales experience, in 2018 I transitioned at work into a new journey in Europe, whereby my role was to transform our sales team members' skillsets and abilities into a new level unseen in our industry. We wanted the best training to enhance the best skillsets and capabilities for our sales members throughout Europe, the Middle East, and Africa (EMEA). My new title was leading "sales improvement" and, initially, the intention was for me to create a new sales manual for our international sales team members. I then spent

four months conducting internal investigation into what sales training and curriculum existed within our organization, what job
descriptions and roles were available and how were they written and
what sales tools and systems were available to achieve our sales goals
and objectives. I realized quickly that what we had was not what we
needed to effectively improve us, let alone to differentiate us from
our competition. As a result, I started on another new journey in
helping us to find what would be deemed truly transformational.

The new adventure was in the shape of a going to university and
participating in a pioneering sales master's program that was a work-
based study curriculum with a mix of academic in-person instruction
and virtual sessions. The primary research was completed during my
work, whereby my focus group of participants were my global sales
team and our business-to-business (B2B) customers. It was here
during this time of work and learning that I gained a new understanding of how to lead a global sales team through transformation
rather than the current public lens of sales improvement or sales
enablement.

This program was offered through the Consalia Sales Business
School of London in partnership with Middlesex University of
London. I chose to go on this journey after some extensive persuasion
by my work supervisor. The opportunity was solid because, as previ-
ously mentioned, I could not find a suitable curriculum for me to
create an internal branded sales manual in guiding our sales members
on how to perform in their roles within any of the sales areas. We had
literally thousands of pages of tips and tricks and product training
but nearly nothing that could support territory management, account
management, sales support, or business development. Our contact
centers had the most abundant training, yet it was still focused on the
consultative sales tips, tricks, and techniques of the 1980s, all designed
to manipulate the conversation and overcome the customer's objections and close the sale. While we said that we cared about the
customer, and I believe truly that we did and still do, we were not
teaching our salesforce anything new in this new era. The training we
had was primarily focused on product training in support of sales
and selling our products to our B2B travel customers and their

business-to-consumer (B2C) customers. In essence, the guiding principles and foundations of sales through science and psychology were absent. It was my executive coach, Brian Tilley, who introduced me to the program that would forever open my eyes to a new world of selling. And that first step required massive change to occur within me.

My initial response was that there was no way I was going to go to university at my age. My supervisor, Stuart Leven, was our vice president and managing director for all of Europe, the Middle East, and Africa. He had more faith in my abilities than I had myself. Together with Brian's help, they convinced me that I could do it. I was a product of the US Navy. I served my time onboard the USS *Carl Vinson* (CVN 70) in the Southern Watch operation towards the end of the Gulf War. While I did go to military schools and became a licensed air traffic controller, formal university at that stage in life was something I had never thought about. Once I got over the initial surprise of going to school again at 46 years young, I discovered that I actually quite enjoyed it and witnessed myself excelling through my work-based research courses.

I told myself that I needed to think of going back to school as if it was a work project that I was building and working on from scratch. For many years I have worked within the world's leading cruise brands and it's something I love doing. Within my current organization, I have become known as a builder of new departments and projects. In 2019, just prior to the pandemic, we had just over 75,000 employees spanning the globe, serving our guests memorable vacation experiences each day. My personality always has been one of curiosity and I am always asking myself how we can do things better. That curiosity has led me to create the industry's first office of Diversity & Inclusion, whereby over 3,000 of our land-based employees were participating in employee groups, making us a better place to work. This opportunity opened so many doors and connected me with leaders within corporations such as American Airlines, United Airlines, Hyatt Hotels, Marriott Hotels, Florida Power and Light, The United States Coast Guard, and Florida International University. I even travelled to the headquarters of the Central Intelligence Agency (CIA) on several occasions to work with their diversity team as well.

My sense of curiosity has also led me to completely overhaul our onboard future cruise program, where onboard our ships we had just one person whose job was to sell future cruise vacations to guests while they were currently on a cruise. Now, through transforming the business operations, we have the most luxurious and profitable travel centers onboard our combined fleets, with multiple sales staff members onboard each vessel, generating a cumulative sum of nearly $1 billion annually during normal business times outside of a global pandemic.

That same curiosity led me to my latest body of public works in starting a new department of sales transformation, where I am now able to help transform our sales teams and champion their personal and professional development across our international division using the lessons learnt from the sales master's program. But my learning and sharing with my sales team members has not stopped solely with the lessons from the master's program. It has only continued onward with the sales leadership lessons I have expounded upon through my doctoral research in leading sales transformation through scholarly and work-based action learning.

What inspired me to create a new personal change model?

The question I've often been asked is: why the need for a new change model? Simply put, I found that the other models were useful and valid but were designed for organizational use rather than personal and individual use. I asked my professors in the sales master's program, "Where is the change model that is designed to help me navigate my own personal change?" Most models that I was introduced to within the sales master's program were for organizations to use on the individual to champion the organization's own change needs. But they do not ask the individual about their own feelings, rather the organizational models assume that the individual will feel or behave in a certain way. I asked myself, "Where is my own personal choice being considered in these models to guide me in my own feelings towards the change? More importantly, am I just supposed to ignore my own feelings and execute the change for them?" Therein lies the gap, and the gap is that I believe these prescriptive models, although brilliant, have a distinct purpose. They are not designed to help the individual with their own personal needs. And because of my new understanding about these change models, my professors advised me that I should go ahead and make my own model. That is exactly what I did. I created the new personal change model that was based on energy and time and focused on the fear generally associated with personal change regardless of whether it is positive or negative.

Until I started my learning journey with the pioneering sales master's program, I had never really thought about personal change or what it meant. I never challenged existing change models that my organizations have used on me in the past. I just assumed these were the right models and that change is just something that will always happen. But since beginning this experience in learning about sales transformation, I have come to a new understanding about leading and managing change.

I have learnt that change is constant and it's personal. How you manage it makes it bearable and achievable. Think about that for a moment. What does personal change mean to you? What does it mean to sales team members that may be under your care? Or perhaps your colleagues and friends? Have you ever initiated a change process at work with your sales team and asked your team members, "Are you ok with this change?" or perhaps maybe you asked, "What does this change mean to you?" Better still, have you asked them, "Are you onboard and will you support this change?" If you have not, can you ask yourself why not? If we know that people act and react to change in variable ways, how do we know if the changes we instill or propose will be accepted and supported by the very people we expect to carry out those changes? And if you are a sales leader and not actively trying to determine who on your team is a change advocate or a change detractor, you might want to have a rethink about that. After all, your role involves leading your employees through change and not just merely telling people to disregard their own thoughts or feelings about change.

Making an impact

Let me ask you this question: Do you believe that an individual has the ability to accept or reject change? If no, then I hope this book will provide evidence on the contrary and challenge your thinking. If you are thinking more critically about change already, as I can safely assume you are since you chose to pick up this book, then I ask you to consider the personal impact every change makes on your team, their lives, and also their performance.

Changes to reporting, sales incentives, organizational structures, territory assignments, promotions, KPIs, and targets can directly impact the effectiveness of your salesforce. Leaders can transform their sales management practice by leading salespeople through personal change, and this valuable skillset can be learnt. Seeing the salesperson as an individual human being, with the ability to accept or reject the changes you impose, will enable you to become a more humane and inclusive leader for yourself. It also will give you the ability to champion your own sales members and provide them with valuable insight in how to manage change for themselves. When we value our sales employees as people who can make their own decisions regarding change rather than just order takers or hunters or farmers or other cute sales titles of the day, we then start to see the values behind the person and can begin to lead and develop in a more intentional methodology that puts the individual at the center of focus. Our goal in leading salespeople should always include their own sense of individuality and personal development and to do that we must look at leading change in a different way.

Transforming Sales Management will highlight how our sales environment itself has changed over the eras and identify who ultimately has that source of competitive advantage. We will then begin to uncover the importance of learning a new way to manage personal change not only for ourselves but for our sales teams as well. This new methodology comes in the form of a model called SCARED SO WHAT. I will take you through learning what personal change means and its new definition. I will share how to give yourself permission to stop and critically reflect what is happening to you during a personal change scenario, through learning and reflecting on change using the SCARED model. Use this new framework to reflect on all types of change to make sense of the emotions driving a potential response. Then, ask: So, what? What does this change mean? What can be done about it? That is where the SO WHAT model can help you to answer those very questions and allow you to formulate your own SO WHAT action plan.

Transforming your sales management style must include learning how to lead yourself and your sales team members not only through the daily routine and tasks, but through change, every step of the way. As sales leaders at organizations, we have invested thousands of dollars, time, and energy into developing our sales team. In the United States alone, nearly $70 billion is spent each year on sales training and education programs (Cespedes and Lee, 2017). Yet, what is there to help salespeople learn to navigate personal change? It is time that we stop and ask ourselves as sales leaders to confront change and help our salespeople navigate what comes with it. Learning how to lead ourselves and others through transformation requires that we embrace this not only from the organizational side, but also from the individual perspectives of team members. Being inclusive and incorporating everyone's viewpoint on change can make us all more productive and improve our ability to transition change faster, while formulating better team unit cohesion and provide for better employee health and wellbeing.

Why sales transformation?

I am not a fan of using the terms "sales improvement" nor "sales enablement" as a defining reference to a person whose job function is to lead the sales team through education, training, sales tools, and skillset advancement. I struggled to find an acceptable meaning and definition of what those terms meant to me. When I created my role back in 2018, initially my leadership called it sales improvement and it kept getting confused with sales enablement by other leaders and team members themselves. Quite honestly, no one on the salesforce knew what it meant. Yet it seemed during this time frame that sales enablement was all the buzz in the sales community outside of our organization.

Sales improvement is often credited to the improvement of sales-people's actions and or activities through formal work measurement. But it is more than just the salesperson's actions. It also includes sales promotion, advertising, and direct marketing (Sarayreh, Khudair, and Barakat, 2013). My new role was not meant to directly manage sales promotion, advertising, and/or direct marketing. Therefore, I couldn't justify using that title as a definition of my role and respon-sibilities. It involved much more than that. Locke, Sirota, and Wolfson (1976) also clarify that the success of sales improvement can be improved productivity; however, employee morale can deteriorate if the sales quotas, targets, or key performance indicators are unrealis-tic or unattainable. For me, this has a direct correlation to the sales employee's ability to understand and manage personal change items and events for themselves.

Sales enablement is academically referred to as deliberate sales learning through three pillars, identified as knowledge codification, knowledge certification, and knowledge articulation. This is facili-tated in sales organizations through a deliberate sales practice and results in measured sales performance (Keeling, Cox, and de Ruyter, 2020). The confusion I face with the definition of sales enablement is that it is often misused to be more focused on the sales tools and commercial metrics of the sales team rather than that of deliberate sales education for the sales members themselves. More often I find that the salesperson or individual is taken out of the matrix of sales enablement.

What I learnt through the sales master's program, my research, and my practice was that to transform sales team members' performance and practices, there must be a larger focus on leading change for the sales team members themselves (Consalia, 2019). That is why I decided to embrace leading "sales transformation" as my title, role, and responsibility. To facilitate this focus, I had to learn not only the science and psychology behind sales but also about the major change models that exist in the world today to facilitate leading change. Korn Ferry (2022), a globally well-known consultancy expert on sales and leading sales, dedicates an entire web page with abundance of resources and consultancy in supporting sales leaders and organizations in adopting towards sales transformation. Gartner (2022), a global think tank and data researcher with annual revenues of over $4 billion, has serviced organizations across more than 100 global communities for the past 40 years. Their 2022 publication, looking at sales as a function in 2025, dominates that sales transformation is the sales process of the future. Consistent change and ever-evolving sales processes are the main focal points of discussion. And the list of global data researchers and trends continues onward in supporting this trajectory towards embracing and managing change.

Where does sales management and change management sit?

This is a very interesting topic—sales management and change management. Where do they fit into the responsibility of salespeople and sales leaders? It really depends upon how you look at the management practices of sales.

According to Tan (2006), change management is defined as "a way to transform organizations in order to maintain or improve their effectiveness". In fact, in my own master's research on this very subject my literature reviews kept guiding me that change management is a methodology geared towards supporting and fostering organizational change processes. And that is where I learnt about how to incorporate all of these models that I will share with you in this book. They are a valid aspect to be included in the practice of managing sales. They are important and they are necessary to help guide us into managing the organizational change that our members go through and experience. But already I have uncovered that neither sales management nor organizational change management focuses on the needs of the individuals who are expected to carry out the changes we impose upon them. And there is the opportunity, which is why I created this new model to aid in the management of personal change. Sales management should encompass leading transformationally and include the personal care and support of our sales team members. That is also my responsibility as a sales leader. And it can be yours too if you read on and learn how to practice it.

In this book, we will dive deep into change management and navigating what comes with the complexities of change for our sales members. The lens through which we will explore change is focused on the kinds of changes that a sales manager would need to communicate to sales teams, offering insight into what goes into conversations amid changes and how to work with your team through these even after changes have been implemented. As a sales leader, you will learn how to help your team manage these often-stressful changes.

Regardless of whether you are working in sales as a leader, supervisor, sales representative, account manager, or whatever role you may have in the sales career field, you are confronted with and involved in change on a daily basis. Changes at work can impact not only the professional life of an individual, but it can also bleed into their personal life. There is no escaping change. In the early chapters of this book, you will learn about the top global change models that are used in modern business today. I will respectfully challenge those models by asking readers to consider the individual: "What about the individual and their own ability to accept or reject change?" In looking through the main global change models, we will learn how best to use them and what they were designed to be used for.

Once we uncover those models and learn about them, we will then take a journey into learning about the individual, and what is personal change and why it is important to learn how to manage it. We will focus on the individual and their own abilities to accept and reject change as it relates to organizational change, which is so often referred to at work or in today's global communication setting. In doing so, my aim is to highlight the importance of the individual and their inherent right to foster a choice about change as it occurs.

What will we learn from these next chapters?

In reading onward, I will take you on a learning journey to bring the element of change management into sales management and transform the way we think about change and personal change, for not only our salespeople, but for ourselves as well. We will learn about the top eight change management models that I think are critically important to help sales management leaders learn about implementing and supporting change within the sales organization. I will then go deeper into why the sales individual is so critical to the success of the organization and where my focus on them is founded. From there, I'll move into how we can support our sales members to learn to manage personal change by using and practicing the SCARED SO WHAT model.

In Chapter 1, the first model we will learn about is Kurt Lewin's Change Theory, otherwise known by many as the freeze model. This model has been referred to as the foundation of change models (Cummings, Bridgman and Brown, 2015), and it is commonly known in psychology today as the basis for assessing change. It is simple in design and upon initial viewpoint, but it is far from a simple process of navigating your way through the change process itself. This model is applicable in referencing the daily process of change we might experience in a sales environment, both internally and externally with our B2B and B2C customers.

The second model we will learn about is from global change leader Dr. John Kotter. His model is the 8-Stage Change Model and has eight steps or stages to navigate one's way through when implementing a change process in a corporate or organizational environment and structure. This model breaks down the stages in which to look at or review the change process. However, it takes the actual change situation further to put it into bite-size chunks to help someone understand and navigate their own way through a change process within the organization. Kotter later amended his model and provided clarity when he released his book *Accelerate*. It was here that he shared that the model was not linear but needed to be followed in a systematic process. However, people, like change, can go back and forth and revisit steps independently.

The third model we will review together is the ADKAR® Change Model. This was created by Joseph Hiatt, the founder and president of Prosci, the change management corporation. The model itself is simple to remember, to identify with, and to use. The majority of information found on the Prosci website reflects how it is to be used within the organization by the organization on behalf of its employees. That said, it does take into consideration the individual by sheer design and is a valuable model in supporting change methodologies. The steps in ADKAR® are Awareness, Desire, Knowledge, Actions, and Reinforcement.

The fourth model that we will learn about in Chapter 1 is McKinsey's 7-S Change Model. This model is 100 percent designed to be used in organizations and large-process structural changes. The very words used within the model promote a business, governmental, or academic setting. I am certain that it can apply to almost any large-scale change or structural process. The key here is that it is to be used on planned changes whereby a strategic governance must be followed.

In Chapter 2 we will continue onwards to the next four models in my top eight. We will start to look more at the personal side by looking at the fifth model that originates from Dr. Elisabeth Kübler-Ross in her 5 Stages of Grief® model, also known as the Change Curve. While this model was created for patients experiencing death and dying, the model and her work has been morphed into the business community for many years now. It has evolved into the sixth model that we will explore together known as the SARA Curve. This is the model that I have discovered is highly referenced to within the sales and business communities.

The seventh and eighth models we will uncover together come from someone I hold in high regard, Daryl Conner. A brilliant change management leader, he created the positive change curve and the negative response change model that we can easily identify with in a business setting and even in a personal setting.

In Chapter 3, I will introduce you to the new era we are actively participating in and selling from. Dr. Julian Birkinshaw has defined this new era and also shows us where the source of competitive advantage comes from. Within sales, this is a critical moment for us to begin to understand the world in which we are now operating and selling from. Customers have changed and so has the art of selling. We must also evolve and learn how to lead our sales members through selling in this new era.

Chapter 5 is where I focus on the importance of the individual sales member. This is where I incorporate change management into sales management and foster a new transformation that each and every one of us in sales must consider if we want to advance our career pathways. There is no escaping that the sales individual is a key critical element that we must pay more attention to if we are to advance our organizations and secure competitive advantage and growth.

In Chapter 6, I will introduce you to the SCARED SO WHAT model. Here is where I will share its origins, design intention, and use, and introduce to you how the sales individual has an inherent right to accept or reject change. As a sales leader you need to pay special attention to this fact, or you are merely leading transactionally versus transformationally. People can reject change ... and some do this silently, while others do it very vocally or with their feet marching out of your door. It's time to learn to incorporate personal change management into your sales management practice. I will teach you how if you continue to read further.

Chapter 7 is critical because it teaches us about the gap between informed decision making and the actions necessary to implement and carry out change strategies. This is where assumptions are typically made and forged, and without a proper action plan or roadmap to guide the individual through change, they can easily fall back into uncertainty or indecision or even begin to reject the change all together. Think of this chapter as the glue that binds the change thinking part together with the change action part.

In Chapter 8, I will take you through a journey that you will not find in any other existing change management model. Once a decision has been made about a change occurrence, people are often left standing and asking either themselves or you as a sales leader these final questions: "So, what does this mean?" or "So, what can I do about it?" And that is where the back half of SCARED SO WHAT becomes so critical: SO WHAT! This is where you will learn to take the common practices within business and strategy and marry them with personal action points to see a change process through for the individual involved.

Chapter 9 will take SO WHAT to the next level and share with us examples of how to create and utilize a SO WHAT plan within the sales environment. We will then uncover how SCARED SO WHAT can also be used as a coaching tool for sales leaders to begin using in their daily one-on-ones and sales practice to further develop their team by asking open-ended questions with the model in the front of their minds. Imagine using sales coaching and incorporating personal change all together. Now that is transformational!

Chapter 10, my final chapter, guides us in how I have used the model within my sales practice and for myself as a leader of sales transformation. I then will share with each of you how you can access the model to use for yourself. I've also created some important tools that you can launch immediately to your sales team members and even for yourself right now, today. And I'm giving you those tools for your use free, for you to begin influencing and transforming your practice immediately.

My goal through this book is to take you through learning about personal change and why it is important not only as a sales leader but as any sales member to be able to learn how to embrace personal change and learn how to manage it. By introducing you to the main change models you will most likely encounter in your work life and then giving you the SCARED SO WHAT model for managing personal change, you will have real world sales examples and understand how to incorporate personal change management into your sales organization. And by demonstrating how SCARED SO WHAT can be used as an effective coaching model, you will be able to help guide your sales teams and foster their creativity for themselves. Coaching is a valuable skillset that is a feature of being a transformational sales leader in developing sales skillsets, talent, and capabilities in creating the next generation of sales leaders. You won't want to miss out on learning these valuable career insights and tools to take your sales career to a new level.

How real is this? Do I use this myself?

Creating the SCARED SO WHAT model has been incredibly freeing to my own personal sense of wellbeing and professional growth.

Across the globe, SCARED SO WHAT is being used not only by my sales team members but also within our B2B customers. It has even been expanded into everyday use and practice by individuals outside of sales and throughout not only my organization, but other corporations and external individuals as well. But I often am asked if I use the model myself and within my own family. Simply put, the answer is yes. But I do remember the most important time in using the model that literally saved my career and sales future.

During the Covid-19 lockdown, I was living in Barcelona and leading sales transformation at our offices there. Our teams were spread across all of the United Kingdom and Ireland, throughout Europe, the Middle East, and Africa. While I used the model for almost all of our sales teams as they were going through traumatic change in losing their jobs, I hadn't really used it on myself... at least not yet. It was our last day living in Barcelona. The office was now shut down and all of the team members were dispersed. They had received settlements and salary continuation through their local governments or had made other arrangements to ensure their survival. Unable to remain in Barcelona to work, I too had to pack up my home and family and relocate back to Miami, Florida where our office headquarters were located.

I was so focused on all the details in shutting up the house in Barcelona and ensuring that everything was done so that we could fly back, that I never really took any time to focus on my own needs throughout this massive life-changing moment. During a global pandemic that caused turmoil for so many, we were not left unaffected. My husband and I made our way to the airport with all our bags in tote and our family cat secure in her traveling case to make the long journey home to Miami. The voice in the sky said, "*Damas y caballeros, ahora estamos listos para abordar el vuelo 1527 de American Airlines con servicio directo a Miami, Florida. Todos los pasajeros de la zona uno deben embarcar en este momento.*" Followed in English with "Ladies and Gentlemen, we are now ready to board American Airlines flight 1527 with nonstop service to Miami, Florida. All passengers in zone one should board at this time."

I never really stopped to think about what I was feeling or how this change was affecting me. I was merely following the direction of my leadership and that was to support in closing the office, transitioning on the salesforce and local teams, and then moving myself back to Miami. My focus was on my family and ensuring everything was getting done that needed to be. It was very much a transactional approach but in a thinking fog. We sat down into our assigned seats and got our cat all secure underneath us so she would be safe for the journey. The flight attendants made their final announcements and checks and a few minutes later we taxied and took off. Looking out the window for the final time at the city of Barcelona and our home, I was filled with immense sadness. The pandemic's claws were sharp and deeply wounding. It was so sudden and so unexpected.

I put my head back in hopes to rest a few minutes and as I sat there, I started to look forward versus just looking at what had happened. And that's when it hit me like gunfire. The shock and impact was like a bullet straight through the heart. I leaped forward and yelled out rather loudly, "OH S#(*T! We're flying into a trap!" The flight attendant looked directly at me and sat forward and asked if I was ok. Shocked and dazed, I looked directly at my husband and repeated, "We are flying into a trap!" He told the flight attendant I was fine and then tried to shush me a bit. The weight of the changes hit me all at once. I managed through closing the office and support-ing all of our sales team members through the transition of losing their jobs. I was so focused on them that I completely forgot that in the United States there is no salary continuation or job protection. Sure there's unemployment, but nothing like what is offered in Europe, and certainly nothing that could support our current way of life. Panic had struck and it all came to the fore that now, we were faced with the results of leaving Barcelona. My supervisor at work was leaving the company soon as well. I was going to get a new supervisor in Miami who didn't know anything about what I was doing. The head office was also closed, and in the United States, they were also letting many people go as the cruise industry came to a complete shutdown. I was certain that I was going to lose my job the minute I returned to Miami. We were flying into a trap, plain and simple, and there was no way out of it.

To find out how this story ends, you need to read onward and learn through my journey! I share it with you freely and ask you to trust me. My journey is not so different from your own journey and perhaps if you read onward, you'll be able to see for yourself how you can shape your own future and career and learn to manage personal change. You are worth the learning investment. It changed my life, and it can change yours too.

01

Four popular change models

Lewin's Change Theory, Kotter's 8-Stage Change Model, Hiatt's ADKAR® Change Model, and McKinsey's 7-S Change Model

One important thing I have learnt throughout my life is this: change is constant; it's personal. How you manage it makes it bearable and achievable.

A salesperson is consistently experiencing change at a very rapid pace. Some changes are forecasted, and others are ad hoc and can come without warning. A typical day in the life of a sales representative includes changes from within the organization to drive sales results and generate revenue. Likewise, a salesperson can experience changes for themselves as a result of change driven by the customer, whether it is in a business-to-business (B2B) or a business-to-consumer (B2C) environment. Change is a constant variable for the salesperson no matter what industry, products, or services they are required to sell. So, we then ask ourselves, what change models are available to support the organization and the sales member?

Life has taught me that, throughout all of the changes we have experienced, change is most certainly personal because of the response required by an individual to interpret those changes and their impact. How we decide to act or react to changes can make them bearable, unbearable, or eventually achievable so that we continue to thrive. One thing I know for certain is that, as individuals, we have the ability to accept or reject change when it involves us personally. And regardless of our own decisions, an outcome will eventually occur.

But it is up to us to decide what the result of that outcome may be in how it affects us individually.

So, the question at hand is this: How can we manage personal change? Before we try and answer that question, I want to share with you the top influential change models that I have experienced personally and have been guided and coached to learn and to use in managing change in my academic studies and professional career. My goal is to put the major change models into one resource for a reader to be able to review, become familiar with, and decide for themselves how they might wish to use them. Further on in Chapter 5 I will then introduce a personal change model designed exclusively to guide the coach or the receiver into critical reflection, then to recognize personal choice and promote action as a part of managing personal change.

From major businesses to universities and to governments and everyday use, people have embraced and utilized popular change models to effectively manage change for organizations and sometimes for themselves. These models are heavily referenced throughout academia and in business practices and come with countless case studies of usage throughout the world. A simple online search for "change models" may yield thousands of results, but the models mentioned in this chapter will be in the top results of your search page.

What kinds of changes are a salesperson exposed to, you ask? Well, there are countless types of change scenarios—possibly far too many to imagine. A salesperson is a broker of sorts. A communicator, a negotiator, a therapist, and a social phenomenon. They should be experienced and empowered listeners who think quickly on their feet but are empathetic and caring in their chosen career profession. They should be strong in their convictions but flexible and adaptable and able to work well in agile situations. Salespeople should be 100 percent authentic and always think and act with the customers' best interests in mind. They should be helpful and offer creative ideas and support to benefit their customers' wants and needs. And they should be so authentic in their sales approach that if they do not have the products or services their client needs at that moment, they should tell them and maybe offer guidance on where they could go to get what they want or need. Does that sound like a salesperson you have met? Maybe yes, but for many, maybe not. Either way, one of my main goals is to help professionalize sales as a career pathway. In my book, our salespeople can and should possess these skillsets.

But when it comes to all of this, the key skillset to have is to be agile; to embrace and practice emotional intelligence to support the ever-changing landscape that is sales. The changes that a salesperson endures each and every day are the very challenges brought on from two main factors:

- **Factor 1: The organization itself.** In a daily effort, much like a boxing match, organizations juggle back and forth between the operations side of the business to the revenue management side and then between sales and marketing. This is not to mention human resources, the supply chain, and now more than ever, government regulations and data privacy protections. Interdependent upon each other, not a single day goes by that everyone is in full sync and processes go off without a hitch. Often more so than not, someone might be behind schedule, or the revenue generation is not meeting expectations. Therefore, the salesperson is often caught within their own wheelhouse trying to navigate constant change in the products, services, or offers and promotions they are armed with to do their job of generating profitable revenues.

- **Factor 2: The B2B or B2C customer.** If everything goes smoothly and the engine that is the organization is running at full speed in harmony, the salesperson will have all of the tools, offers, promotions, and necessary wherewithal to offer their customers both service and support in successful selling. That said, our customers are human as well. And they too, like us, have their own side of operations, sales, service, supply chain, human resources, and so on that are typically involved in the decision-making to buy products or services. In the cruise industry, our B2B travel customers are typically independent from our cruise brands. This means they run their own businesses and we are selling our cruise inventory to them. They have the ability to sell us or to not sell us on a daily basis. They have their own budgets, timing, ways of working, and ways of supporting their end customers. If their schedules, timeframes, and operational needs do not align with ours, then we have massive change scenarios that our salespeople will find themselves smack in the middle of, trying to negotiate between the B2B customer and our brand as the supplier. And that's on a good day! Now throw in the economy, weather, politics, a global pandemic, and the environmental impacts to local markets and you've got a whole other lot of change scenarios to reflect on.

Going back to the notion of change being constant and personal, the key to making change manageable and achievable is utilizing change models. And to help make change manageable and achievable for our salespeople, we have some change models to support our journey along the way.

Kurt Lewin's Change Theory

Kurt Lewin (1890–1947) was a German American psychologist famous for his contribution towards social, organizational, and applied psychology in the United States (Lewin, 2021). He named his model the "Change Theory." The model is a three-step process whereby you identify a change that is needed, freeze it, and make the change, and then re-freeze to embed the change process (Figure 1.1). Some people might say that the model itself may appear as quite simplistic and outdated for today's constant change society. However, it still represents a foundational aspect and approach to facilitating change.

FIGURE 1.1 Lewin's freeze model from Strategies for Managing Change website, operated by Stephen Warrilow

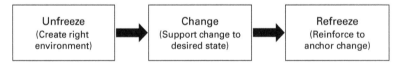

SOURCE Image recreated and used with permission from Stephen Warrilow.

It consists of three phases or steps. Lewin's direction and intention for using this model was to bring about planned change for groups within organizations and societal levels. The stages are, in the simplest terms:

1 **Unfreeze.** In this step, you review the current behavior or process that is the subject of being changed and stop or discontinue that

situation or practice. This can be a complex task but is often the process review stage looking at what it is that is occurring now and no longer suits the needs of the organization. Thus, at this stage, discussions should be held and an agreement made to discontinue the current working methodology or framework.

2 **Change.** In this step you implement the new process or methodology. This is known as facilitating the change. It is here where the people involved will action the new working methodology or framework and set up the new ways of working.

3 **Re-Freeze.** In this step, you solidify the new way of thinking, working, process, or practice and move forward. This can be done by groups or individual encouragement, coaching, mentoring, or constant reminders of the new process. In order to make the change effective, all participants must be agreeable to the new process and enacting the new way of working.

We can assume that this process was designed to be implemented within group settings for a change process that was intended to be introduced. Sarayreh, Khudair, and Barakat (2013) discussed that by their own design, unless the group norms and routines change, individuals won't change their own behaviors. We can further assume that Lewin did not design the model to be used for personal change as the written focus was on the organization.

Before using the freeze model, one might want to review the current situation to determine if a change process is warranted. Lewin created two supporting mechanisms for this purpose, first introduced in *The Principles of Topological Psychology* in 1936 (Householder, 1939). The first is "Lewin's equation," which is not a mathematical model to use explicitly but rather a heuristic formula to represent a rule-of-thumb in human behaviors. The equation is represented as $B = f(P,E)$, where B is equal to Behavior and F is equal to Function. P represents the Person involved and E is the Environment in which all of the change would occur. It was in this formula that Lewin affirmed that behavior is a function of the person representative of their environment. The formula represents the individual's perspective of the situational change, and this is the larger focus and key to understanding their behavior versus simply relying on their past experiences.

Lewin's second foundation in managing change with his freeze model is to utilize a tool he created called "Forcefield Analysis." This is a simple whiteboard analysis whereby the change leaders would do a pros and cons brainstorming session (Warrilow, 2009). In this scenario, one lists out the pros and cons of the proposed change with the change itself listed in the middle. Pros on the left; change in the middle; cons on the right. For each pro and con listed a score is given to each item. Typically, one can assign a scale of 1 to 5, where 1 equals little driving force and 5 equals significant driving force. At the end, all the scores are tallied, giving a tool to help decide the outcome.

If the outcome is favorable, then one might decide to press onward, which is when the freeze model can be utilized to begin the process of implementing organizational change. I believe that Lewin was trying to create a framework to reference the change process itself. If people want to make a change to an existing process or procedure, they will need to freeze it and analyze what the "it" is, and then make the change to the new normal that they are wanting to put into place. Then they re-freeze and solidify the new process so everyone can move forward with the new normal. His model describes the overall process of change management to use within an organization.

I can easily see this model being used during everyday sales processes across organizations throughout the working environment. An example would be in how we look at territory or account assignments and allocations for salespeople. We could easily freeze the current process, look at what needs to change and make that change, and then re-freeze and execute our new territory assignments. That is a simple example of how we might use Lewin's model in sales. For that matter, how many of us have taken out a marker pen and gone to a whiteboard to list out the pros and cons of doing something? I have done this many times with my sales teams and other departments that I have led throughout my career. It may be with a marker and a board or through a virtual session on Zoom or Teams where we facilitate a breakout session. I may not have known at the time that I was doing a change forcefield analysis, but the principles of looking at the change process were there and, for that, I can say Lewin's tools and model are applicable today.

As a sales supervisor, leader, and educator, in my career there have been many times that as a sales team we met together and said, "Let's reflect on what we are doing right now." This process forces managers to stop and take a look at what is occurring, then pause and freeze the current actions involved in the working process and flow before moving onward. In its most simplistic terms, one might say we use Lewin's freeze model all the time, as we should credit his work at any time that we conduct a brainstorming session that generates steps worth implementing. We just might not have known who created it. Can you reflect on ways that you might have used this change process within your sales practice?

Kotter's 8-Stage Change Model[1]

Next, let us look at a popular model from John Kotter. His work in leading change in a business setting is acknowledged globally, and he is an author and researcher that I respect greatly. John P. Kotter has served as a professor of leadership, Emeritus, at Harvard Business School and is an author as well as the founder of the Kotter International (Kotter, 2021). He is someone that I hold with high regard in the art of managing and leading change. One of his most popular models is the Kotter 8-Stage Change Model (Kotter, 2012), which he introduced in his book *Leading Change*. You can see the model here in Figure 1.2.

As Kotter is a leader in business and organizational change management, his model was designed for use in organizations for known change processes that the organization wanted to put into place. He created this model with the intended use of leadership or, more specifically, change management leaders within an organization, whose roles include bringing about and implementing change.

The stages in the model that the leader or change management team would need to go through are listed in eight individual areas.

FIGURE 1.2 Kotter's 8-Stage Change Model

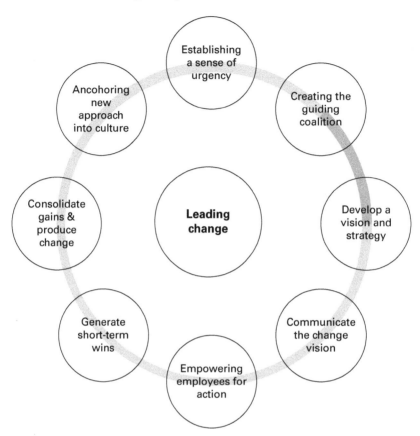

Step one is where you create a sense of urgency. In step two, you create a core coalition to work together. Step three is where that coalition works together to develop a strategic vision. In step four, the vision plans are shared with others to gain team visibility. Step five is where the leaders involved in creating the plan begin to empower employees to take action. Step six looks to generate short-term wins for the change process. Step seven is where leaders consolidate gains and produce changes within the organization. And finally in step eight, the change is initiated.

During the first step, you want to create a sense of urgency in and aligning on the necessity for the change. For the change to have meaning and impact, Kotter suggests that three-quarters of the leadership should be onboard with the change. As a sales manager, you should also be prepared to explain this change and answer any question about it. Anything less than a three-quarters majority can lead to the change process faltering and having a negative impact. In doing so, make sure this is supported with evidence via tools available such as SWOT analysis (strengths, weaknesses, opportunities, and threats). Use all the strategic tools available to analyze the current market and or competitive environments to support the need for change. Therefore, the leader or leaders and members must be on the same page and agree that the change needs to occur in the first place before moving forward.

In the second step, the leader(s) will want to create a core group of people that will lead and execute the change process within the organization. Here the main responsibility is for the group to drive and maintain the sense of urgency, support, and guidance. This group should be made up of people from across leadership levels to ensure the momentum is maintained and supported. This group's responsibility is to drive through actions and support of the organizational change needs. Kotter places a great amount of focus on creating and maintaining this sense of urgency. This is the key to driving change success.

In the third step, the leadership will want to develop a clear vision and strategy for success of the change process they are implementing. It is here that due focus must be given so that, whatever the change is that needs to occur, it is clearly written and easy to articulate. This means that they must be able to communicate, in one or two sentences, the importance and overview of the change intended to occur. Failure to have a clear vision means that the team members who are tasked with facilitating the change will quickly lose focus and attention. They must be onboard with the change and be able to share the key aspects of the change in full clarity.

In the fourth step, Kotter directs that you need to share the vision and communicate at every opportunity. This goes much further than just sending an email. It is here that he suggests that any major change opportunity must be done in a face-to-face setting at the first stage. If it is to be perceived as important and the sense of urgency observed, then it merits a face-to-face setting. Once that has occurred then follow up communication has to be supported. This can be in the form of email or print communication, but it is better if the leaders and core group tasked with leading the change follow up in personal communication with the people involved in executing the change. The key here is to communicate in a meaningful and impactful method. Do not just send an email and expect the change to occur.

The fifth step is about empowering employees to facilitate and execute the change strategy on behalf of the organization. This moves well beyond the initial stages of planning and preparing for the change process to a new stage of implementation. Here, the change leader's role shifts away from planning to facilitation. This is done through empowering the team to execute. During this time, you continue following up and giving support, creating a sense of urgency, but you listen to your employees and take on data points of progress for the change process at hand. Your role may be to remove any barriers that are preventing the change from occurring and that can include people who are blocking the change process as well. In this process the change leader(s) may find themselves in a position to coach and guide change blockers into change adopters.

During the sixth step, the change leader or leaders will generate short-term wins. It is here that, as you maintain your sense of urgency throughout the process, you celebrate those change adopters that are creating short-term wins. It is important to maintain a sense of motivation and movement by rewarding and recognizing those that are championing your change process towards success. The goal should be to create these opportunities for employees to facilitate short-term wins. In doing so, the praise that comes along with these wins will be visible to other employees involved and they will want to join in the movement as well. People like to win. People enjoy recognition. This should be the easiest and most rewarding part of the change process being implemented in the organization.

The seventh step is to consolidate gains and produce the changes desired. This is not a time to celebrate too early. Champion those small wins and victories. However, do not let off the drive for the overall change process. Do not stop the sense of urgency. Rather, at this stage you want to regroup with the leaders involved and assess what has occurred. Ask the members what has worked, what has not worked, and what needs to happen next if the change is going to be successful. This is a time to regroup and refocus. If a change in participants is needed, then regroup and make those changes in team members or structure to ensure that you bring the overall change process into play. In essence, don't call victory too quickly. It can fail just as fast as it can succeed!

The eighth and final step is to initiate the change itself. This can also be similar to the re-freeze part of Lewin's Change Theory model. It is the stage in which you implement the new ways of working into a new normal. The change leader(s) is not done. Far from it. There is too much at risk for things to return to the previous ways of working. In fact, this is a time where the leader(s) must continue the praise and comparison of business success versus the prior ways of working. This can be done through continued praise and celebration of business wins with employees and consistent communication on the new progress. This establishes the new working culture and framework of working.

I do believe that using these eight steps as a mechanism to implement a major change could be very beneficial. For our sales team members, "we" have followed this model in its full conception when implementing a new organizational sales structure. Prior to 2021, our international sales teams were not globally aligned with the same core job functions, titles, roles and responsibilities that would suit our modern B2B customer needs. Therefore, through active research and consultation of internal stakeholders and external sales leadership guidance, we utilized this model as a framework for implementing our global reorganization into a new working structure. This process was a year-long process that was carefully and strategically thought out, and by the beginning of 2022 our new change process and organizational sales structure was in place to serve our guests as we came out of the global pandemic. The 8-Stage Change Model serves as a process guide and roadmap with eight points to check during the change process. It is easy to get distracted with driving a change process within the organization because one still has their main full-time job to achieve sales targets, and drive sales promotions and activities that will produce results.

FIGURE 1.3 Kotter's eight accelerators for leading change

The everyday work pressures do not subside just because you are implementing a change process.

It is important to note that Kotter later came out with a revised version of the 8-Stage Change Model in 2014 with a book called *Accelerate* (Kotter, 2014). In Figure 1.3 you can see that he advanced and clarified his model into a fluid eight-step process for leading change. The items are similar but in essence he has new learnings from the implementation of his model to modern business.

In Figure 1.4 from the same source, Kotter describes the differences between his original model and the newly adapted version.

FIGURE 1.4 The differences between Kotter's models

There are key differences between John Kotter's 8 models		
8-STEP (*Leading Change*, published 1996)	&	**8 ACCELERATORS** (*XLR8 Accelerate*, published 2014)
Steps are positioned to be used in a structured and sequential method in responding towards change	⟷	Accelerators are succinct and continuously operating
The steps are typically driven by a small group of people, but they hold power	⟷	Accelerators incorporate as many as possible throughout organization and propose to formulate an army of volunteers
The steps are created to function and be utilized within a traditional structure	⟷	Accelerators require agile methodology of working within a network

SOURCE Adapted with the permission of Harvard Business Review Press. Left: From *Leading Change* by John P. Kotter, Boston, MA, 2012, pp. 44–45. © 2012 John P. Kotter by the Harvard Business Publishing; all rights reserved. Right: From *Accelerate* by John P. Kotter. Boston, MA, 2014, pp. 44–52. © 2014 John P. Kotter by the Harvard Business Publishing; all rights reserved.

As a sales leader, I appreciate the changes that Kotter has referenced in this setting because he is acknowledging the rapid pace of change while also adding clarity in the intended use of his model. Many people take models literally, so he has done a great job articulating that this process is not meant to be rigid or linear. Years ago, we might have looked at his model and thought that the change process he outlined would be owned by the leader exclusively. Now, we view the business leader as a change sponsor who is helping larger teams in an organization manage change.

Hiatt's ADKAR® Change Model

This next model has a significant twist to it. It involves something that is not articulated with the models we have covered thus far. ADKAR® (see Figure 1.5) is one of the very few models that I recognize was designed and intended to include the personal side of change. It was created by Jeffrey M. Hiatt and first explained in his book, *ADKAR: A model for change in business, government, and our community* (2006).

FIGURE 1.5 Hiatt's ADKAR® Change Model

SOURCE Adapted with permission of Mohan Karambelkar and Shubhasheesh Bhattacharya, from "Onboarding is a change: Applying change management model ADKAR to onboarding", *Human Resource Management International Digest*, 25 (7), pp. 5–8. © Emerald Publishing Limited 2017. Permission conveyed through Copyright Clearance Center, Inc. Special note: PROSCI®, ADKAR®, and AWARENESS DESIRE KNOWLEDGE ABILITY REINFORCEMENT® are the registered trademarks of Prosci, Inc. Used with permission. Prosci, Inc. is not affiliated with, and does not endorse the content of, this publication.

Hiatt is the founder and president of Prosci®, the change management corporation. His creation is a five-step model that he instructed people to use in his proposed order to achieve success (Hiatt, 2021; Creasey, 2022).

ADKAR® is designed around two core principles. The first principle is that it is the people that change, not the organization itself. Without the people to facilitate the change, the organization will not change on its own. The second principle is that successful change will occur when the individual change matches the stages of organizational change. To facilitate this, Warrilow (2009) states that both the individual and those leading the change from the organization will utilize the steps in ADKAR®.

The steps in order of usage (Karambelkar and Bhattacharya, 2017) are as follows:[2]

1 **Awareness** of the need for a change. In the first instance the individual or employee needs to be aware of the change. This is not to be confused with the awareness that the change is happening but more for the awareness of why the change is occurring.

2 **Desire** to participate and support the change. This is a hard decision as it is a personal one. Does the individual have the desire to participate in the change?

3 **Knowledge** on how to change. This is the individual having the knowledge of what to do during and after the change.

4 **Ability** to implement required skills and behaviors. Creasey describes this in his video as the capability or ability to do your job

differently. Can you demonstrate the ability to do the new process in your work? You are following the new processes or using the new tools for change.

5 **Reinforcement** to sustain the change. There are tendencies to revert back to the old ways of doing things. Reinforcement is the ability to support the change going forward.

The organization will achieve change success when the individual changes progress at or close to the same rate of progress throughout the change process being introduced at the time. Prosci® have provided a definition of the business dimension of change which includes typical project-based elements of business needs and opportunities identified to projects that are defined to include scope and objectives. They further include that from these workstreams new processes and systems are developed and solutions are implemented into the organization.

Prosci® further advises that once you apply ADKAR® to a "non-work change" then you can begin using it at work. While there is no additional commentary that I could uncover, I believe that they are referencing a non-work change to be a personal change that occurs outside of work. I assume they want you to practice using ADKAR® in your personal life and then come to use it within your work life. However, this is not clear and is just my assumption. Joseph Galli (2018) also refers to Hiatt in referencing the use of the model exclusively in a work-based environment. For the model to be successful, the desire by the employees must be there to provide motivation towards the other stages in the model. And continuous reinforcement would be needed to ensure the change is embedded in the organization.

I appreciate that ADKAR® refers to individual needs and they are including the individual as being an important element in their change design plan. The effort for inclusion is here and stresses the importance of the individual being core to the success of change. I have had many discussions with the change management leader within our organization. His role is established specifically within our human resources division to champion and support the overall business units with change transformation, tools, and resources. His preferred model to use for overarching business change needs is ADKAR®.

In 2020, when we were at the end stages of our new international sales organizational design phase and were ready to begin implementation, I partnered with our change management leader in human resources on the communication aspect of the new global organizational structure. Immediately, he began to recommend and articulate how we could follow the ADKAR® principles to communicate and create the awareness of the change process. He then further guided that it would be up to us as the business unit leaders to champion the support of the individuals to ascertain if they had the desire to make the changes along with the sales organization. Once we understood and could confirm the individual sales members' desire to participate and embrace the change, we then needed to support them with the knowledge in championing their ability to make the change process happen. And finally, we worked on the plans to ensure that we could reinforce the new organizational model and facilitate a new culture and structure that embraced organizational change. It took an army both within the leadership and the sales members themselves. But the good thing is that by using both Kotter's 8-Stages model and ADKAR® together we were able to implement the new organizational sales structure with our international employee population.

Overall, the global sales employees on our teams accepted the structural design changes and began to adapt and work into the new organizational roles and levels that we created for them. There were a few people that resisted the changes being implemented and challenged the need for them. However, the greater majority understood and went along the journey in a rather peaceful and impactful way. There was no disruption of service or support within the sales teams themselves, nor to the B2B and B2C customers we serve.

ADKAR® also has the ability to support sales members on their daily journey and work process. As they are experiencing rapid changes coming both from within the organization internally and from the B2B customers externally, it is almost as if they are like a ball being rapidly bounced around from side to side—like in a pinball game. ADKAR® has the ability to be a tool used either by the individual or by the sales leader to ask questions and seek understanding.

An example from our cruise industry sales environment could be something like this. A travel customer (B2B) does not have the marketing funds available to promote a weekend special cruise fare that our brand wants to offer. As a sales leader I can seek to understand if my sales account manager has an awareness (A) of what they might be able to do. I can assess if they have the desire (D) to find a solution to support both the business needs of promoting this weekend special cruise offer with the travel customer. And I can also ascertain if my sales account manager has the knowledge (K) of how to think this through to the next steps leading towards actions (A). My role is to support the sales account manager to manage or create and foster solutions between our sales teams and our customers. I can use ADKAR® to facilitate that staged process thinking. The final phase would be to support my sales account manager with the reinforcement (R) of their abilities. In this situation, I would prefer to use a sales coaching method along with ADKAR® to allow the sales account manager to critically reflect on what they think they could do to support a positive outcome for all involved. I know what answer I would choose, but if I tell them, then there is no facilitation of learning. My goal would be for the employee to create and own the ideas and situation themselves. In this instance, our industry solution would be to supply the travel customer with co-operative funding to help them secure the marketing opportunity they need to promote the weekend sale. It helps the travel customer and our business to win together. But the real learning and development is the ability to use ADKAR® to facilitate a change process to a successful business outcome.

McKinsey's 7-S Change Model[3]

This next model is for certain intended for business or organizational use. But it is one that is highly visible, and you may come across it in your working life, so it is important to have it in your resource library should you need to use it. Let us take a look at McKinsey's 7-S Change Model. From the beginning, you can possibly see that this popular model for change is intended to be utilized by an organization or on a major project. The very words themselves are designed towards those references in business or organizational use. McKinsey's 7-S

FIGURE 1.6 McKinsey's 7-S Model

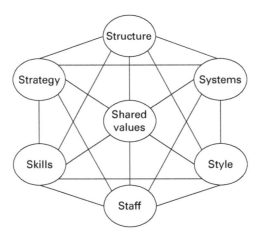

SOURCE Used with permission of Robert H. Waterman, Thomas J. Peters, Julien R. Phillips, from "Structure is not organization", *Business Horizons*, 23(3), pp. 14–26. © Elsevier 1980. Permission conveyed through Copyright Clearance Center, Inc.

Model, as seen in Figure 1.6, was created and designed by Tom Peters, Richard Pascale, and Robert H. Waterman Jr while they were working as McKinsey employees in the late 1970s (Channon and Caldart, 2015; Galli, 2018).

It was created as a tool or guide in understanding or diagnosing organizational issues and concerns and to formulate processes for improvement. In the late 1970s there was an increase in frustration of executive leadership related to the strategic and organizational structures in place. The model they created to look at these strategic and organizational structures was a series of talking points that were designed to be interdependent upon each other. These cohesive elements are called the seven Ss.

The seven Ss are illustrated by Channon and Caldart (2015) and I have elaborated on the meaning by extracting upon the explanations and research provided:

1 **Strategy:** What is the strategy necessary to fulfill the desired objectives? Meaning: strategy represents the set of actions that the organization will do as a result of or in anticipation of changes in its operational environment and structure. If successful, these

actions should enable the organization to meet or exceed their goals and key performance indicators towards a successful outcome.

2 **Structure:** What structure or people do you need to facilitate the project? Meaning: structure is the viewpoint of looking at the existing people and processes in place. In this stage, one will evaluate the structural processes and make recommendations based on market, geographical locations, and operational needs to support the organizational change or shift.

3 **Systems:** What systems will be included for design, monitoring, and control? Meaning: systems represents the actual processes and procedures, tools, and functions that are in place today. What are they? What and whom do they serve? Which are realistic and which could be changed or altered? Take a look at how the organization truly works versus what is written in policy and procedure.

4 **Skills:** What distinct capabilities of the staff to fulfil the strategy are needed? Meaning: in this stage, one will look at the skillsets and capabilities that are in place today versus those that are needed to make the desired outcome in the future once the change structure is implemented.

5 **Staff:** Who will be included for motivation and support? Meaning: in McKinsey's 7-S Model, staffing was considered to go beyond the normal hard and soft issues. Hard issues represented salary and compensation structures, and appraisal systems and soft issues represented employee morale, engagement, and overall employee wellbeing. The framework is inclusive to recognize that employees must be nurtured, developed, and recognized as integral to the success of the organization rather than the organization by itself.

6 **Style:** What will be the leadership style for the project and team? Meaning: this is concentrated on the senior leadership involved with fostering the overall change. Do they have a hands-on approach? Are they micromanagers, transactional leaders? Or do they lead differently all together? An agreed approach to management style is necessary to ensure successful outcomes.

7 **Shared Values:** What common beliefs and values will guide the project? Meaning: at the core of McKinsey's 7-S Model are the shared values of the people involved with executing the operational strategy and processes at hand. These values are what the organization pivots around and embraces as a whole. If the change in play is significant enough, it may require the organization to shift or change its own values, and to be successful they must include the shared values of all members.

I appreciate this model because it is mindful of the individuals as well as the organization. The inclusive model itself takes care to point out the significance of the staff and their own values in relation to those of the organization. This model is intended to be used on implementing major transformation or change in a workplace, organization or large project setting. A leader in sales might find themselves using this type of model for large-scale changes such as a departmental reorganization, new sales leadership implementation, post-pandemic evaluation of working processes and procedures, evolution of the sales business structure, or items that are being sold.

The creators of McKinsey's 7-S Model also cautioned that the success in using this model for change within the organization is dependent upon the successful adaptation or acceptance of the new shared values between the organization and those who work within it to execute the strategy and overall success (Channon and Caldart, 2015). This is an important factor, and it makes me ponder if an employee's own acceptance of the change being imposed is taken into consideration in one of these 7-S stages? As a leader in a working environment, be it in sales or any other aspect, I would want to know or have some indicator if an employee accepts or rejects the change that the organization is imposing. Or are we just hoping it will be successful? Without knowing this information, we may have employee disengagement or, worse, they may leave. And we for sure do not want that to happen.

In the next chapter, I will take you through four more popular models that I have experienced within my work environment as well as within my academic studies. Again, my goal in sharing these models of facilitating change with everyone is to open their minds to the ability to foster change not only for oneself or their organization but for their salespeople as well. After all, they are typically the ones within the organization under the leader's charge and care that have to execute the vast majority of changes imposed. Therefore, if one wants change to be successful, then it is incumbent to learn the tools available in managing and executing change to its fullest potential.

Endnotes

1 Permission to include Dr. John Kotter's models granted by the Harvard Business Review Publication Corporation.

2 Adapted with permission of Mohan Karambelkar and Shubhasheesh Bhattacharya, from "Onboarding is a change: Applying change management model ADKAR to onboarding", *Human Resource Management International Digest*, 25 (7), pp. 5–8. © Emerald Publishing Limited 2017. Permission conveyed through Copyright Clearance Center, Inc. Special note: PROSCI®, ADKAR®, and AWARENESS DESIRE KNOWLEDGE ABILITY REINFORCEMENT® are the registered trademarks of Prosci, Inc. Used with permission. Prosci, Inc. is not affiliated with, and does not endorse the content of, this publication.

3 Used with permission from Channon, D. and Caldart, A., 2015. The McKinsey 7S Model. Granted February 2022.

02

Four more change models

*Kübler-Ross' 5 Stages of Grief®, SARA Curve,
Conner's positive response curve, and Conner's
negative response curve*

In the last chapter, we uncovered four very mainstream models that someone might come across in their professional careers when working within an organization or with a change management process or change professionals. The next four models I would like to discuss with you are models that you have most likely encountered in some form or fashion. In any event, no matter if you have experience with change models or have no experience at all, these models are more tapped into the responses of the individual confronting change than the others. How the models are or have been used is a different story, however, and we'll talk about that more in Chapter 4. For now, I ask you to keep an open mind to review with me and learn about four more models I think are globally relevant.

The 5 Stages of Grief®, or The 5 Stages of Loss® change model

The fifth model that I would like to share with you comes from an individual who is sadly no longer physically with us but lives on through her legacy of helping others. Her name was Dr. Elisabeth Kübler-Ross. She was born in Zurich, Switzerland, one of triplet sisters who grew up to join the medical field and specialize in supporting terminally ill patients with coping with their impending reality on death and dying (Ross and Rothweiler, 2022). In her career she worked in many different hospitals but was horrified and repulsed about how terminally ill patients were treated. She devoted her career and research with terminally ill children, AIDS patients, and the elderly to support the stages of personal grieving and acceptance of the patient's situation while facing death. A founder of the hospice movement and author with over 20 published books and academic contributions, she was catapulted into the spotlight with her book *On Death and Dying* (Simon & Shuster, 1969; republished as Kübler-Ross and Byock, 2011). In her book, she revealed her conversations with patients, and her own reflections of those conversations, and depicted the eventual stages a terminally ill patient might go through towards facing their own death. The mainstream depiction of this model is known as The 5 Stages of Grief ®. Let us take a look at these stages and what they mean:[1]

- **Stage 1—Denial:** In the denial stage one might experience or express thoughts of disbelief. Thoughts like: "This cannot be happening," or "This does not mean what I think it means," or "This will not affect me."

- **Stage 2—Anger:** During the anger stage, there is a sense of understanding and possible acceptance or rejection of the situation at hand. This causes frustration and turns into anger. The person may react in a negative state and not be willing to listen to reason or any sort of comforting messaging.

- **Stage 3—Bargaining:** This stage represents causation, where the person involved is trying to seek alternative solutions: "Could I do this, or could I do that?" or "What if I could have some more time?" The process is a way of rationalizing or trying to come to an understanding of the possible outcome.

- **Stage 4—Depression:** In this stage the overwhelming weight of the situation at hand comes to reality. The person's mood and comfortability factor sink to a low point, causing depression. They are thinking or expressing words like "This cannot be happening" or "I cannot believe this is happening to me".

- **Stage 5—Acceptance:** In this final stage a form of acceptance occurs whereby the person is adjusting to the inevitable outcome they are facing. This could be a process described as "coming to terms" or "accepting the inevitable" and giving into the resistance and letting go of hope for a different outcome.

Looking at Figure 2.1, we can see where these five stages occur throughout the experience Dr. Kübler-Ross described from her conversations and discussions with patients. I find it very interesting that hope is illustrated across the stages up until the final moments.

Dr. Kübler-Ross' model has also been depicted in this popular line graph that we can see in Figure 2.2. In this line model, we see the stages that have been expanded to capture Shock, Denial, Frustration, Depression, Experiment, Decision, and Integration. All of this is based on her original book, where she shared her 5 Stages of Grief®, also known as the 5 Stages of Loss®, or just the 5 Stages (Kübler-Ross and Byock, 2011). She identified these stages as elements a patient might go through in the process to react or cope with dealing with a great situation of loss, grief, or a shock to their being.

FIGURE 2.1 Kübler-Ross' 5 Stages of Grief™

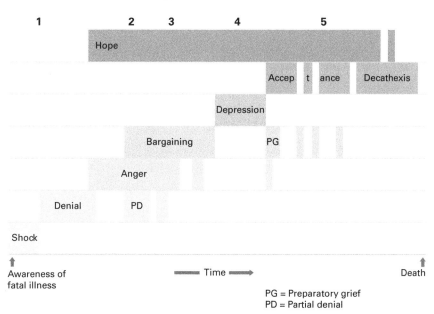

SOURCE Used with kind permission granted by Elisabeth Kübler-Ross Family Limited Partnership. (https://www.ekrfoundation.org/)

FIGURE 2.2 The Kübler-Ross Change Curve

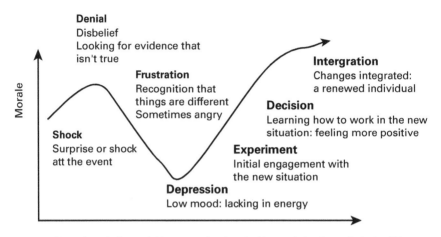

The Kübler-Ross Change Curve ®

SOURCE This trademarked material is recreated and used with permission from Elisabeth Kübler-Ross Family Limited Partnership. (https://www.ekrfoundation.org/)

Both of these figures illustrate that there are more elements than just five simple stages a person might experience through death or the process of dying. However, I think there is one benefit from using this model in a sales context, despite the obvious fact that it wasn't designed for us to use this way. The stages can be used at random, so long as they are all covered. I know this to be true because I was so very fortunate to sit and take the time to talk with Ken Ross, the surviving son of Dr. Elisabeth Kübler-Ross in September 2020 in a virtual interview.[2] Ken Ross is the president of the Elisabeth Kübler-Ross foundation and together with his sister Dr. Barbara Rothweiler, they lead the foundation to keep their mother's work alive for all to continue to benefit from and utilize. In my time with Ken, he shared how his mother created her model and what it meant to her and what she was trying to achieve. I found it profoundly disappointing how many people across the globe have chastised or criticized her work but never taken the time to ask or find out how she intended the model to be used.

It wasn't meant to be a model at all. Moreover, it was a framework to facilitate a discussion. In her original book she described the 5 Stages of Grief®. Critics quickly tore her work apart and said that she missed the sixth stage: hope. But, if you read her book, there is an entire section on hope. Somehow some people (mainly critics and skeptics) have completely missed this gem. In truth, her work was never intended to be a structured research program nor a methodological process of collecting data in a research setting. Her work was conducted through discussions, conversations, observations, and reflections upon these sessions with patients who were dealing with impending death and dying. Dr. Kübler-Ross' work uncovered 13 stages, but that was too much for people to digest so she kept it simple around the five condensed stages for people to be able to facilitate a conversation. She also never intended for it to be reviewed as a literal structured model. In my interview with Ken Ross, Ken mentioned that his mother said that "people may or may not experience all the stages. They may skip some or not experience them at all." He further shared how she wanted to create a framework for a discussion and that this was the culmination of her experiences in facilitating what it was to deal with death and dying.

Continuing my discussion with Ken, I could not wait to ask him one final question. And that was this: "Did your mother create or know about the SARA or SARAH Curve?" In all my research during the sales master's program, I could not locate a true source of creation for this version of her change model. Every reference directs that the original creator was Dr. Kübler-Ross. I finally was going to find out the long-awaited answer and directly from the closest person to Dr. Kübler-Ross who would know the answer: her son. He informed me how he knew that people from the business community had reached out and inquired with his mom about the usage of her 5 Stages model within the business community. She acknowledged that the model could be used for anyone experiencing great loss, grief, or dealing with shocking change situations. She said that people could use it for instances other than death or dying. She just wanted it to go past the literal stages and facilitate conversation. And, no, she did not create the SARA nor the SARAH curve model. Ken does not know who officially adapted his mother's model into this popular business version of the 5 Stages.

While the 5 Stages of Grief® have provided an amazing model for people to facilitate a conversation surrounding death or dying, Dr. Kübler-Ross understood that her framework was being adapted and utilized for many widespread circumstances involving change. She knew that it had made its way into the business community as well and that it had been adapted to the SARA or SARAH curve. Let us take a closer look at the adapted version of her working model.

The SARA Curve

In Figure 2.3, we can see the SARA Curve and the different elements that it refers to (Rogel, 2010). In this instance we see the following elements

FIGURE 2.3 The SARA Curve

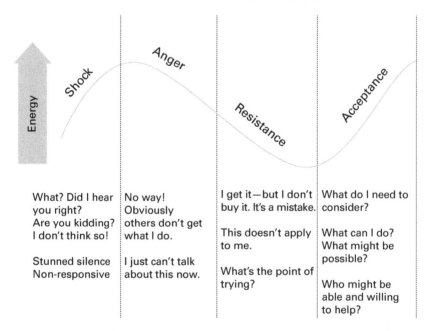

Reactions to Feedback: SARA Model

What? Did I hear you right? Are you kidding? I don't think so!	No way! Obviously others don't get what I do.	I get it—but I don't buy it. It's a mistake. This doesn't apply to me.	What do I need to consider? What can I do? What might be possible?
Stunned silence Non-responsive	I just can't talk about this now.	What's the point of trying?	Who might be able and willing to help?

SOURCE Used with permission of DecisionWise, from "The SARA Model: Learning from 360-degree feedback" by Charles Rogel.

that are being utilized in a business setting. Here, Rogel refers to the SARA Curve for an employee receiving feedback after participating in a 360-degree survey-based feedback program. This is a popular program that is used within businesses and organizations on developing leaders.

In each stage of the SARA curve the elements are depicted as follows:[3]

- **Shock:** Shock represents the initial reaction to the situation at hand. In this element a person might display shock with verbal statements or personal thoughts similar to "this can't be right" or "I don't believe this". Typically, these are the initial feelings as a result of a change process or, in this instance, feedback from a 360-degree evaluation on them performed by others.

- **Anger:** On absorption of the change process at hand, the next stage could result in refusal to accept the change, or the information being forced upon them. This can put the receiving person in a situation of anger. It is a negative response in disbelief or not willing to accept what is happening. For this situation in dealing with the results of the 360-degree evaluation, the person is expressing anger as a form of non-acceptance of the feedback they were given.

- **Resistance:** Resistance can come from the discussion or unveiling of the change after anger passes. This can be in the form of the person experiencing the change saying that they like things just the way they are. Change is uncomfortable for many people, and they may be unwilling to change their attitudes, personality, abilities, or processes. In this instance, the person is not willing to adhere to or listen to and absorb the feedback and recommended changes suggested in the 360-degree feedback.

- **Acceptance:** This is the final stage in the SARA Curve. At least, for this version of it. Here the person has made the journey through initial stages of shock, anger, and resistance and are now finished with their defiance towards the change itself. They have moved on and decided to accept the change at hand. And in this circumstance, the person has received and overcome their anxiety and frustration with the results in the 360-degree feedback program and has embraced the changes necessary.

While it is not listed on this version of the SARA Curve, there is an additional letter representing "hope" that comes at the end of this model. It is less widely used but, nonetheless, it does come up from time to time in business change processes. Hope represents the ability for a person to embrace the new change situation and trust the process will lead to a favorable outcome.

Regardless of whether Dr. Kübler-Ross created the SARA or SARAH Curve versions, she started a movement in her field of study and work that has transcended her original intentions. Her work was based on patients dealing with death and dying, but it has since been adopted and applied across the globe into corporate and organizational change management structures and is still being utilized to this very day.

Earlier, I said: "Change is constant, it's personal. How you manage it makes it bearable and achievable." That is what is happening here. People have grabbed onto Dr. Kübler-Ross' 5 Stages model and have adapted it for their own use in business or organizations and even in personal situations. One can clearly see the similarities between the SARA curve and the 5 Stages and the Change Curve models depicted by Dr. Kübler-Ross. In essence, her desire to facilitate the conversation has come true, and people are talking about it throughout all walks of life.

No matter whether it's SARA, SARAH, or the 5 Stages of Grief®, people are yearning to find a way to manage change and deal with the outcomes that occur from change constructs within our lives. In a sales environment, I have come across the SARA curve many times. From sales training courses, to managing conflict at work, to workplace harassment, to rolling out new programs ... the SARA curve founded on the principles of Dr. Kübler-Ross has been a staple in trying to antic-ipate how sales employees, and all employees for that matter, will process the changes we as an organization impose upon them. I am confident that you will come across this popular change model at some point in your professional career. Hopefully though, you will now have a better understanding of where the SARA Curve originated and what its initial function was designed to achieve.

In our everyday sales careers, no matter if you are a front-line employee, sales representative, manager, or the chief sales officer, you will be affected by change on a daily basis. Take, for example, the weekly trading meetings or revenue meetings within your organization.

Every company has someone focused on the numbers. And it is from within this department that the direction of the sales force is generated. If we are exceeding our revenue generation, then the revenue leaders will ask for more. If we are falling short of our revenue targets, then you can be certain that they will be asking for more… if not demanding it. This brings about change and impacting change situations on a daily basis. There is a popular phrase among sales professionals that says, "You are only as relevant as your last sale," and that sale needs to be often and fresh daily.

Salespeople will have considerable pressures that come from within to achieve goals, but they will also face change scenarios from their B2B or B2C customers. Imagine that a sales account manager has been working for over a month to try and secure a new business account. The amount of work involved can be countless hours at all times of the night and day, working to resource the needs of this new account, and to understand the business financials and the vision, mission, and goals of the business customer. The account manager will surely be working to foster new connections and generate a working relationship. At the same time, they will be brokering back and forth between their organization for the products and services and pricing elements to align with the new potential account's needs. And then they would be aligning that with what the customer wants and expects. This is a normal process for an account manager or a business development manager and at the same time they may be managing other existing accounts to maintain the sales cycle of winning, maintaining, and growing their pipeline and business opportunities.

Now imagine at the end of this month-long negotiation process, just when the account manager feels the customer is ready to sign a partnership agreement, the account comes back and says, "No thank you." They end all communication, cease to answer any emails, or return any phone calls and drop off the communication chain all together. If you are this account manager's supervisor, what do you expect they will be feeling or experiencing? Could you use the SARA or 5 Stages model to reflect on their situation? Of course, you can. We're human after all. And if you are a positive leader who champions coaching and or transformational leadership principles, you'll consider how the employee is feeling due to the situation at hand.

They will potentially be in shock, with confusion and disbelief, and constant questioning of what happened and why the sales communication fell through. They might experience anger. In this situation, they might shut off completely to a learning or coaching development opportunity. They might be casting blame on others or even to you as their supervisor or to themselves. As they progress onward, they might resist a supervisor's coaching or attempts to support them. They might resist moving onward to try and secure other new business opportunities or support existing accounts and relationships. This is an important time for a supervisor, leader, or sales coach to check in with the sales member to ensure they can help them think through the process. If they are able to get through, then the sales member might move on to the next stage of acceptance. This is also an important stage for the salesperson because as their supervisor, one might want to understand what it is that they have accepted. Did they give up on the account? Did they move on to source and support new business or existing clients? Or did they try to revive the potential account relationship through the support of others?

This is just one of hundreds of different change scenarios that occur each and every day throughout a salesperson's career path. If one stops and reflects on this example, could they possibly relate and see other examples from their own personal experiences? I believe they can. A question you might be asking right now is, "Why is this all so important?" And then you might ask, "Why do I need to know how to manage personal change?" Keep those questions in mind or write them down. They are extremely valid questions that might be expected at this stage in reading this book. I assure you that I will answer this and make it very clear in Chapters 4 and 7 of why managing personal change is critical to our evolution in managing change.

The positive and negative response curves

The last two models that I would like to enrich your learning with come from the same person. Daryl Conner (2022) has led a career in change management for over 40 years at the time of publishing this book. An active author with two major published works and over 250 contributions to book chapters and journal articles, Conner is an experienced leader in the art of managing change. His goals include helping organizational leaders to recognize that change is necessary to have a positive impact and experience for their employees. And he is an avid supporter of other change professionals championing their own practices in leading and supporting change management. I can confirm this to be 100 percent true, as I reached out to him for his review of my personal change model and to incorporate his models for managing change. He was very responsive and supportive as his profile states on his LinkedIn account. I have great respect for his prior work, his change models, and his continued work in championing organizational change management practices.

In 1993, Conner published *Managing at the Speed of Change: How resilient managers succeed and prosper where others fail*. In this book, he uncovers two additional models that I found to be very interesting in the construct of managing change. In Figure 2.4, through

FIGURE 2.4 Conner's positive response curve

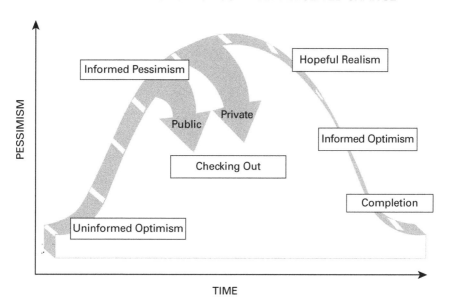

EMOTIONAL RESPONSE TO POSITIVELY PERCEIVED CHANGE

his model, Conner articulates and reflects the journey of a person experiencing a change process via the emotional responses they display during a change process that is perceived to be positive or favorable. Let us now look at each element and what they represent.

In this model,[4] Conner expresses his views from his experiences where he sees people embracing a positive change situation initially but may resist at a later stage:

- **Stage one is Uninformed Optimism:** This is where the person experiencing the change does not have all of the information, but they are hopeful the change process will be positive and therefore are willing to go along with the change process itself.

- **Stage two is Informed Pessimism:** In this stage, they have experience and information about the change process as they are directly involved with it. Conner states there is no way to avoid this stage in the process once people become engaged with the change process. They may be pessimistic about it as this portrays their degree of discomfort, but they are duly impacted and involved with the change itself.

Between this stage and the next are two elements that may occur publicly or privately as a result of their involvement or actions, and they can lead to the person involved in the change process to check out. This is due to a person's tolerance level. If a person can no longer tolerate the change process, they may check out. This is a process where a person withdraws from the change situation at hand. That does not mean they will not return to participate; it just means that they may go dormant in the change process. They might return to the conversation… or might not.

- **Stage three is Hopeful Realism:** This is the stage where a person believes that the change can be manageable or achievable. There is the presence of hope.

- **Stage four is Informed Optimism:** The person involved has achieved information from the change experience. They are optimistic that change will eventually achieve a positive outcome.

- **Stage five is Completion:** The change is complete. The people involved are now able to live with the change in their new normal as the change experienced was perceived to be positive.

In Conner's book, he describes this five-stage change process with an example of a new couple experiencing marriage for their first time together. For our purposes, let's use an example relevant to the world of sales. Think of a new hire key account manager (or KAM), who has just joined your team and comes from an external source outside of your own sales industry. They are fresh and young when it comes to selling your products and services, but they came highly referenced and qualified to do the job. In the beginning everything is perceived to be positive. This is a major change situation and the KAM and yourself as their new supervisor are both forging a new working relationship. That's stage one—uninformed optimism. Neither the KAM nor yourself as leader have concrete evidence nor experience of how this new working relationship will go, but you both are excited about it nonetheless. As you progress into the post-probationary period, both of you realize things are new and different and that each of you must learn how to work with the other. This can be the next stage of informed pessimism. After a little while longer, you both now have knowledge of each other and are amid the change cycle. Pessimism can reflect the level of discomfort with the change process—even though it is perceived as positive. This is a cautionary time for a supervisor and a newly hired sales employee as both have working relationship tolerance levels and if either one of them are breached, then they could check out and the change process may no longer be considered positive.

As the KAM and supervisor continue to adapt to this new working environment, they begin to realize that things might have the potential to work. This stage is the third one and is hopeful realism. The team are hopeful that their new reality will be fruitful. As such, they then transition into informed optimism where they have experience from the transition and change process and are optimistic for a favorable outcome. And finally, they are working through the change process and moving onward. This is the completion stage. Conner uses a newlywed couple as an example to articulate how the positive response to change can occur. I have adapted it towards a sales supervisor and a new hire sales employee to illustrate a common example within our profession. Conner also tells us that this type of example only represents one change cycle. Like the newlyweds in his example and the sales supervisor and KAM in my example, they all will go through this again and again for perceived positive change processes.

But what happens when the change perceived is negative? Conner has modeled this through his research and extensive change career to answer that very question. In Figure 2.5, he shows us what happens when a change process is perceived to be negative. It is important to note, and Daryl Conner asked me to reiterate, that the basis of this negative model stems from the brilliant work that Dr. Elisabeth Kübler-Ross created within her clinical psychiatry practice where she interviewed, and held discussions with terminally ill patients about their journey dealing with death and dying.

On the left axis of Figure 2.5 is emotional response. This is the response the person experiencing the change will portray based on their emotions involved with the experience. On the right axis is time. Change does not happen all at once. There is a time element involved within the process.

Let us explore the model approach further here.[5] The phases one might experience when using this model in a business situation where the emotional response to change is perceived negatively are as follows:

- **Phase one is Stability:** Conner represents stability as the phase that occurs after the announcement of a change process. This phase represents the initial stability or present state the person involved is experiencing.

- **Phase two is Immobilization:** Much like Shock in the SARA(H) Curve or 5 Stages Change Curve, the person experiencing the change can experience shock. This can make the person unable to respond or action the change process occurring. They might be confused or completely disoriented as the change is perceived to be negative.

FIGURE 2.5 Conner's negative response curve

Negative response to change

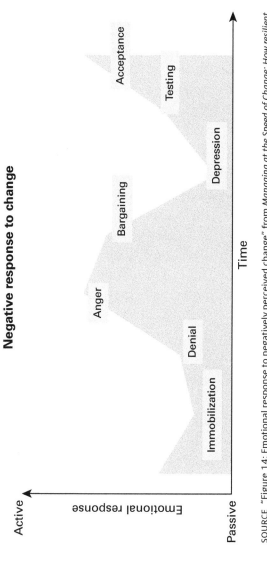

SOURCE "Figure 14: Emotional response to negatively perceived change" from *Managing at the Speed of Change: How resilient managers succeed and prosper where others fail* by Daryl R. Conner, copyright © 1993 by O. D. Resources, Inc. Used with permission of Villard Books, an imprint of Random House, a division of Penguin Random House LLC. All rights reserved.

- **Phase three is Denial:** In this phase of the change process the person involved will be in full denial of the change happening to them. Here, they are not able to participate and may not seem present in the moment. They may flat-out reject the change as introduced or may express their sincere disbelief and denial outright to others.

- **Phase four is Anger:** At this point as the person is experiencing the perceived negative change, they may lash out at others closest to them. They may be expressing sincere frustration, disappointment, or outright hostility towards the change happening. Usually this occurs with people that are closest to them and willing to listen or to people who are within arm's reach and can be recipients of the hostility and anger. Notice this is the same as represented in SARA(H) as well.

- **Phase five is Bargaining:** This phase will mark the beginning process of accepting the negative change. The person involved can no longer deny that it is going to happen or is happening. People involved at this phase will be displaying behaviors and actions of trying to negotiate. This can occur in many different ways. It may be that they are asking for an extension to the deadlines given or asking for other alternative solutions that they perceive as more applicable. This is also represented in Kübler-Ross' 5 Stages of Grief®.

- **Phase six is Depression:** Conner describes this next phase as a normal process and to potentially expect it from the person experiencing the negative change impact. While they most likely would not experience the full term and effects of clinical depression, they will still feel and display an uncomfortable disposition. They might express discomfort and portray the role of a victim by saying, "Why is this happening?" or "There's nothing I can do about it." They might withdraw from their normal routines and workloads, but this is usually a phase that shows they are processing the negative change further.

- **Phase seven is Testing:** When the people involved begin to explore new ideas or possible realities to the negative change, one can sense they are in this phase of testing. They are trying on the new reality and transitioning away from the depression phase. They are searching for ways they can be successful themselves within this new reality.

- **Phase eight is Acceptance:** It is here in this final phase that the person involved with the negative change impact finally resides to the change imposed. They may not like it at all and for some time they may still display reminders that the change was not favorable. However, they are on their way to processing and working within the new environment where the negative change occurred to or with them. This is synonymous with the SARA(H) Curve that was adapted from the 5 Stages of Grief® model. Eventually, there is an actualization of the change, and for the living… they will eventually move on.

So, if the model is so similar to Dr. Kübler-Ross' model, why would he need to create an eight-step adaptation? The answer is simple: things change. Change happens in all types of settings during our lives. Dr. Kübler-Ross created an important foundation with her 5 Stages model and was focused and dedicated on helping terminally ill patients to process the changes they were going through. Conner realized early on in the 1970s that the 5 Stages could be applied into the business community to support organizations implementing change processes through the virtue of their employees. The employees themselves were the action items to facilitate the change. And their experiences towards change in this environment were worth noting and exploring so others could learn how to manage change, whether it was perceived as positive or negative. Hence, the two additional models.

I have said it before, and I will say it again: change is constant; it's personal. How you manage it makes it bearable and achievable. What all these change leaders via their models that I have shared with you in this book are articulating throughout their work is that change is inevitable. We must find relevant ways for us to learn how to manage change versus simply going through the process and experiencing unnecessary anxiety, stress, and fear. What they are expressing as change leaders is that change is manageable if we learn how to face it, break it down, and navigate the process.

More relevant to sales is where Conner takes his two models further and articulates that to manage change, we must first use sober selling as our approach. Here, what he is referring to is that in the early nuances of a change process, we must articulate and inform people what the true costs of the change process are going to be. For example, if the new sales approach is going to require an increased investment in marketing and collateral expenditures, then we must tell them the truth and sell it to them. An example might be: "The result in launching this new marketing campaign is going to bring significant overall returns. No one likes to spend extra money, but if you want to be successful you have to spend money to make money. Let's explore how we do this together." In this instance, I've just told you that we are going to have to spend more money on this marketing campaign. That was truthful. But I've also shared with you that it will also help bring greater returns on our investment and asked you to explore the opportunity with me. It is a way of selling the change through to the person receiving it.

This approach does come with a risk in the fact that since you were honest and told them that they are going to have to spend money to make money, they might not wish to explore that option with you. Remember, they are experiencing the change as well. It is a journey that we often experience in the sales arena. And in my viewpoint, it is better to be honest than any other way. The key here is to understand how people react to change. These models provide an overview and a guide point for you to use to enhance and develop your own experiences.

The next time you are working with your sales team members and are introducing new sales campaigns, taking away marketing dollars, adding marketing dollars, implementing a new organizational structure, or navigating between what revenue management wants and what the sales team can deliver, remember everyone is experiencing change just as you are. Learning more about how people can manage change, act, or react to change can help people navigate a more successful outcome. More successful for the organization, but also for the employees and people involved with the change itself.

During my sales career, I thought that I knew a lot about sales and the sales process and cycle, commercial sales management, and how to manage global sales teams towards successful outcomes. I have been very successful for my organization and myself, but that was not only because of my efforts. It was always due to the collaboration and support of others, and I will always remember that. It was not until I started my journey in 2018 into the sales master's program, Leading Sales Transformation, through Consalia Sales Business school and Middlesex University of London, that I realized there was so much more than just the typical consultative sales tips, tricks, techniques, and array of sales tools and customer relationship management (CRM) systems that constituted sales management. There was this ever-present factor called change. And my role as a sales leader was to know what change meant and how to manage it not only for myself, but also for my sales team members. If I was going to truly transform our sales team into the next generation of highly successful industry sales professionals, I needed to embrace and practice the art of managing change as well. And the first step after learning how to manage it through change management models and processes was to learn that the sales environment, landscape, and working processes also change over time. In the next chapter, we will look at the evolution of sales over time and what sales environment we will be operating in for the next 50-plus years.

Endnotes

1 September 2021 interview with Ken Ross. Used with kind permission granted by the Elisabeth Kübler-Ross Family Limited Partnership, 2022.

2 Unpublished interview with Ken Ross, President, Dr. Elisabeth Kübler-Ross Foundation, September 9, 2020.

3 Used with permission of DecisionWise, from "The SARA Model: Learning from 360-degree feedback" by Charles Rogel.

4 "Emotional response to positively perceived change" from *Managing at the Speed of Change: How resilient managers succeed and prosper where others fail* by Daryl R. Conner, copyright © 1993 by O. D. Resources, Inc. Used with permission of Villard Books, an imprint of Random House, a division of Penguin Random House LLC. All rights reserved.

03

Changes to buying and selling

Snapshot of the effects of the global pandemic

In early 2022, the world was beginning to return to a sense of normality. More or less, a new sense of normal was occurring for whatever individual reality that may be. After nearly three years of living within a global pandemic caused by the breakout of the Covid-19 virus, over 464.8 million cases of the virus were confirmed. These were just the confirmations where medical authorities were able to test and identify the virus. Worldwide, over six million people died after contracting the virus due to complications from Covid-19 (see the WHO Coronavirus Dashboard, Covid19.who.int, 2022). The world continues to change on a daily basis.

Sales and the practice of selling also had to adapt as a result of the Covid-19 virus that wreaked havoc on global societies and the sales environment. People across the globe were forced into lockdowns for long periods of time. This meant that no one, in certain locations and regions across the globe, was permitted to go to their offices or places of employment as a normal part of their working environments. In a global survey conducted through Facebook in 2020, it was identified that the hardest hit industry was the travel and transportation industry where nearly 57 percent of businesses closed (Goldstein et al., 2022). The second highest rating of business closures, at 47 percent, came in the hospitality and event service sectors. This makes complete sense when one factors in that travel came to nearly a full global stop. And for social events, functions, and public outings, well, there were literally next to none that were happening for long periods of time around the world. People were all huddling in their homes and glued to the television and internet for sources of entertainment and information about the pandemic. The next hardest hit area was in education and childcare services where nearly 45 percent of businesses closed. The performing arts and entertainment industry was not able to escape the pandemic effects and as a result nearly 36 percent of businesses closed. The final figures that were tracked show that the global hotel and hospitality industry, including cafes and restaurants, reflected nearly 32 percent of business closures due to the pandemic.

Within my own profession, where in 2018 it was estimated that the total global cruise industry was valued at US$150 billion (KPMG, 2020), we experienced a full and complete shutdown. Every cruise line in the world had to completely stop service. The ability to generate revenue went to zero literally in one month by global orders from government disease and medical guidance authorities. Oddly enough, this did not happen to airlines nor hotels but did so within our industry. The $150 billion dollar valuation is just from our perspective of the ships being able to sail with paid passengers. It does not take into account the ships as hardware, the cruise line employees on land and sea and their earning potential, nor all of the businesses, organizations, cities and ports, and local economies around the globe that the cruise industry supports through jobs, purchasing of goods and services, and the tourism dollars that pour into every place that we go. The cruise industry and its impact far exceed the $150 billion valuation when you take all of this into account. And it literally came to a hard full stop and remained closed for over 18 months. This was a first in history.

As shared earlier, we were not alone in this problematic situation. Businesses around the world were forced to reduce their normal operations significantly or shut down all together. The main effect that came out of the global pandemic was fear and uncertainty. For long periods of time people were forced to quarantine and remain huddled down in their homes. For most, we were able to get out and get groceries and the necessities of life, but even then, those businesses and services that remained open to support their greater communities were faced with supply chain disruption on a global scale. People stood in long lines at the grocery store only to be met with semi-bare or bare shelves with limited stocks of goods to support their needs. Restaurants had to quickly transition away from open dining to making deliveries if they wanted to survive. At first, that was the main option for many months, but trying to keep people employed and working was difficult for families with small children. There wasn't any daycare. So, many just had to stay home and could not work. The effects of Covid-19 transformed the entire world in the way we lived, functioned, thrived, and even our survivability. But after two years of living within the confinements of Covid-19, vaccines became available and as we staggered through the eligibility requirements from being a senior citizen first to protect our elderly population all the way down to children aged 12 and up, we started to pull ourselves out of the effects of this global tragedy. Life as we knew it back in 2019 was starting to return, little by little. But obviously after two years of living and working from our homes or trying to find a way of making a living, the landscape of what we used to value through the normal 9-to-5 work life routine had changed.

Yet, even before Covid-19 had taken place, the practice of sales and selling was already changing and the consultative tips, tricks, and techniques of the 1980s that every salesperson was taught were already starting to become outdated.

The compounding effects of the global pandemic thrust even more change upon the art and practice of sales and selling. Indeed, sales has changed and continues to evolve and change as each day goes by. Dr. Philip Squire is the president and CEO of the Consalia Sales Business School headquartered in London with representation in Singapore as well. He earned his doctoral degree through global sales research in understanding the question of how people wanted to be sold to. He linked this back to the values and behaviors that salespeople display. As a result, Dr. Squire's doctoral research linked these behaviors and values into positive and negative sales mindsets as a way of working and selling. In his book *Selling Transformed* (Squire, 2021), he traces the roots of the art of selling back thousands of years, where the earliest forms or transactions of buying and selling were solidified by the exchange of gold, silver, copper, and even cowrie shells. These early exchanges became the foundation of the art of selling and bartering services and goods. It is fairly safe to say that sales as a career and practice have evolved, because I do not believe that we continue to use these items as everyday exchanges as they did thousands of years ago. And perhaps what they were buying and selling way back then has also changed, but the process of selling itself remains the same. Or does it? Is sales as a profession merely the bartering or negotiation of a good or service between a person who has versus the customer who wants? I believe there is much more to it than just that. Dr. Squire goes much further into the art of selling and transforming the sales process itself. But we'll talk about that and his work a bit further in Chapter 4. I don't want to get ahead of myself just yet.

First, I ask you this. Can we agree that sales and the process of selling faces changes over time? If you answered yes, great! Then let me show you how sales through the sources of competitive advantage is changing. If you answered no, then you really should read on as well and have an open mind to learn something new. It may very well help you as you grow onward and upward in your career and endeavors.

The eras as defined by Dr. Julian Birkinshaw

Dr. Julian Birkinshaw is a Fellow of the British Academy (FBA) as well as the Academy of Social Scientists (FAcSS), the US Academy of Management (AOM), and the Academy of International Business (AIB). He is currently serving, as of this writing, as a Professor of Strategy and Entrepreneurship within the London Business School. He is also the Deputy Dean of programs at the London Business School as well as the Director of the Deloitte Institute for Innovation and Entrepreneurship. His credentials are strong in foundation and his research and experience evidenced. If we take a closer look at how the sources of competitive advantage have changed over the past, Dr. Birkinshaw breaks it down for us and reveals a deeper look at how the world and particularly how each of these sources of competitive

FIGURE 3.1 The eras—source of competitive advantage

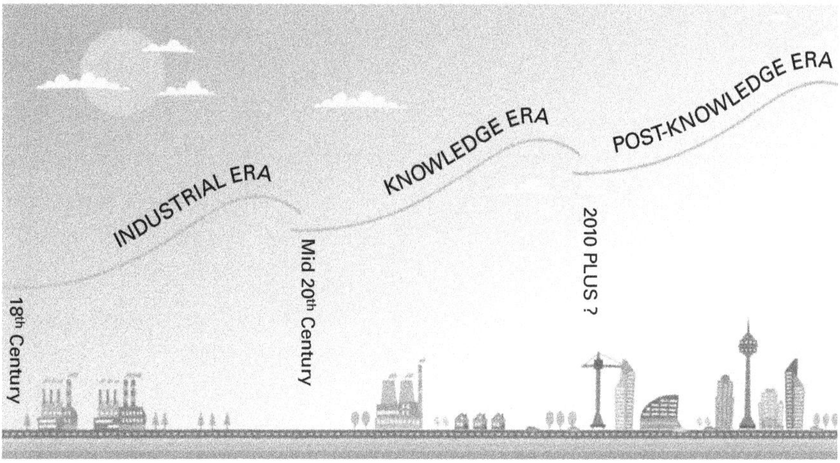

SOURCE Appears in "The ERAS: Sources of competitive advantage" at the 2014 London Business School and Deloitte Global Leadership Summit. Used with permission from Julian Birkinshaw.

advantage have changed over time (Birkinshaw, 2014). In Figure 3.1 we can see the eras in which Dr. Birkinshaw articulates where the greatest impact on sources of competitive advantage have occurred and that when one era ends a new source of competitive advantage is required. What is an era, one might ask? An era is a defined measurement in time. There are several different types of eras, and it depends upon which scientific entity and what purpose in the measurement of time you are referring to. We are currently living in the "Meghalayan Age" according to global geologists in measuring the last 4,200 years (Thompson, 2022). But for more recent units of measure and referencing to business and socioeconomic events, we are looking at eras as measurement of the span of 100 years (otherwise known as a century).

The 18th and 19th centuries: Industrial era—bureaucracy

The late 18th and early 19th centuries are when the industrial revolution took place. This is where we began to transition from a period where almost all of our products and goods to be sold or bartered were made by hand. The industrial era originated in the United Kingdom where they led with mass innovations as historians say around the 1760s and continued into the 1830s and 1840s. The United States would emerge into the industrial era as well and later surpass the United Kingdom and lead the world with innovation and development. During this timeframe, iron making, textiles, and steam and waterpower inventions were the thriving capital products of innovation and creation. The development of motorized tools and processes to create other tools and products was introduced. The vast majority of these innovations were driven by sources controlled or serviced by governments and corporations and organizations that were supported by government. Companies involved within this process of creation, innovation, and ability to compete at the time were the elements that comprised a "bureaucracy". "What is bureaucracy?" you might ask. It is a system or process where the operations of the entities are managed and run by state or government control or influence. It is not an easy process to make change as everything has to be run through the government. Think of Social Security, the Internal Revenue Service or Department of Taxation, and the Department of Veterans Affairs in the United States—all examples of a bureaucratic-run operations.

Back in the 18th and 19th centuries, companies and organizations were mainly forged through government enrichment and thus operated as a bureaucracy. The main source of competitor advantage was forged through the seller and was controlled through government formulation and regulation. Back then, buyers who wanted to gain access to the spoils of the industrial age were less informed and competition was limited. The sellers of these products and services had the upper hand in knowledge, expertise, and the ability to drive the products into mass adoption. The sellers valued return on capital as their main key performance indicator and had control over production, sales, distribution, and the determination of costs and value. The systems and processes were all kept internally as a key source of competitive advantage and thus gave sellers the upper hand in transactions, processes needed to sell, and overall growth. Buyers simply bought without the ability to seek alternative pricing, referrals, or advice.

The 20th century: knowledge era—meritocracy

As we transitioned into the 20th century, a new wave of innovation was beginning. During these early times, items such as the air conditioner, neon lighting, the automobile, the telephone, the electric battery, the powered airship, the typewriter, and even the first mechanical computer were created (Dorling, n.d.). Innovations in the way we lived at home to the way we would shop and buy goods and services began to flourish. More and more businesses were forming, and innovation was breaking away from the earlier days of a bureaucracy towards something new. The ability to compete for offering and selling the same goods and/or services was now taking a wider approach. Entrepreneurship began to flourish, and more and more people were starting and formulating their own businesses. Flash forward to the year 1969 and the internet was born (Web Foundation, 2019). Some would say this was the greatest transformation the world would ever see in this era. And it did just that. The internet transformed the world, and a new breed of technology and industry was just about ready to change the sources of competitive advantage and the way we all worked and lived, yet again.

On April 1, 1976 (April Fool's Day), Steve Wozniak and Steve Jobs released the first home-based version of the computer (Bellis, 2017). Little did they know that this invention would formulate the foundation and main source of competitive advantage for the modern consumer within the knowledge era. With mainstream access to the internet through the new home-based modern computer, which would be copied and replicated by other manufacturers, the consumer was rapidly finding themselves able to have more knowledge and access to data and information at their fingertips.

Dr. Birkinshaw defines this main source of competitive advantage within the knowledge era as a meritocracy. A meritocracy is defined in many ways, but roughly it means that the system of government or running of operation or organization is determined by the people and how they progress based on their merits or ability to contribute via their own physical and mental contributions. Here in this new era, if we focus on socioeconomic abilities, the consumer has the main advantage because they have access to a tool such as the internet, which provides people a global library of referencing and information about sellers and their products and services. The consumer now has the ability to quickly learn the differences between one seller's perspective, offer, and approach, versus that of someone else who is selling the same items and or services. The seller no longer has the main source of advantage as the consumer is armed with knowledge. In contrast to a bureaucracy, in a meritocracy both the consumer and seller have advantages. In the meritocracy, both are using data and information to make themselves more informed. Thus, data and information formulate this key innovation within the knowledge era. Think about tools like Salesforce, LinkedIn, or even Facebook, Yahoo, Google, websites such as Amazon, Walmart, or Target, Expedia, Travelzoo, and Airbnb, etc. All of these tools allow both the seller and the consumer to access and source data, thus generating knowledge. However, unlike a bureaucracy, where the seller has the main control, now the buyer has the main source of competitive advantage. They can force the seller to work much harder in order to compete for the actual sale. Perhaps you might have heard the phrase "Knowledge is power"? Sir Francis Bacon published in his work, *Meditationes Sacrae* (1597), the saying "knowledge itself is power" (Azamfieri, 2016). Many will say that this famous phrase was said much earlier and may even have come from biblical texts. Whoever created it was a genius, because it was coined long before the transition into the knowledge era.

The 21st century: post-knowledge era—adhocracy and emocracy

We are now living in the 21st century. So, what comes next? Are we not still living within the knowledge era? The answer is not so easy to define

FIGURE 3.2 The eras—source of competitive advantage broken down

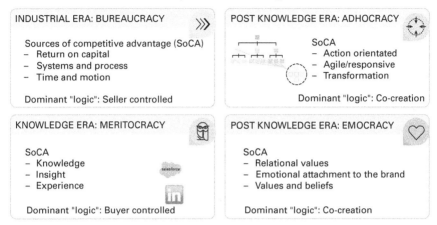

Source of competitor advantage and time

SOURCE Appears in "The ERAS: Sources of competitive advantage broken down" at the 2014 London Business School and Deloitte Global Leadership Summit. Used with permission from Julian Birkinshaw.

but one could say yes for some people and no for others. Dr. Birkinshaw, through his research, says that we have entered into a post knowledge era. If we look at Figure 3.2, one can see the sources of competitive advantage from the industrial era, where inside a bureaucracy, return on capital, systems and processes as well as time and motion were the dominant logic.

This era is representative of creating a seller-controlled environment. As we transitioned into the 20th century, it would become known as the knowledge era. Here, Dr. Birkinshaw describes a meritocracy, where the dominant logic is a buyer-controlled environment. This is led by the more readily accessible systems and process to acquire data and generate knowledge, insight and give consumers the experience to have the main source of competitive advantage. But as each era comes into play, we are seeing that the sources of competitive advantage change as well. In the 21st century, Dr. Birkinshaw says that from about the year 2010 onward, we see yet again the sources of competitive advantage changing. And this time, it has split into two variable directions.

The adhocracy: co-creation

The first point of reference now describes an adhocracy. An adhocracy is a system with flexible rules that is able to change rapidly. It operates as an informal organizational structure and has none of the systems of red tape or blockage that one would find in a bureaucracy. Think of it like a small committee or a project management group. The process is temporary, flexible, and able to make recommendations and act quickly. As depicted in Figure 3.2, in an adhocracy sellers and organizations who are selling products or services need to be inclusive of the ever-changing status quo and each other. With the introduction of computers and internet into the knowledge era, and rapidly expanding in the post-knowledge era with the advancement of artificial intelligence (AI) where machines are programmed to think for themselves, this is also becoming known as the digital era. This rapid advancement of technology with new systems and processes that are artificially running and supporting our livelihood states that "change will never be as slow as it was today". That means that change will continue to affect us at a faster pace than it ever has before—and this affects both buyers and sellers equally. Therefore, organizations and sellers need to embrace this transformation through agility and be rapid in their approaches to embrace the ever-changing sales and service environments we are living and operating within. Sellers and organizations are now co-dependent upon the consumer in order to be successful.

In the adhocracy, people, businesses, and organizations no longer can live and hide under complacency. The new requirement for success is innovation. Failure to innovate means that eventually your business entity or operation will be outdated and subject to demise as others will rapidly advance around you. An extreme example of this lesson can be seen from what occurred within the internet giant Facebook. The social media tech giant has lost US $500 billion in stock value since they changed their name from Facebook to Meta in October 2021 (Corrigan, 2022). That is $500 billion in less than one year. While there are many impending factors that faced this unfortunate reality, one might attribute the main cause towards not being cognizant of the adhocracy and remaining complacent. Google and Apple both introduced significant changes to privacy and security enhancements to protect their customers data. The mood and flow of customers also led a transition away from stagnant Facebook pages where misinformation has been so highly politicized, to consumers favoring social sites such as TikTok. This platform completely changed social media from static posts and pictures to short videos. One might argue that if Meta (Facebook) were focused on agility, they might have had the foresight to see these important changes occurring. As a result of the success of TikTok and the woes of Meta, Mark Zuckerberg had no choice but to bow to the unsurmountable pressure and the movement of the modern consumer. He was quoted as saying that the social media giant was facing "unprecedented levels of competition" as they faced the single greatest loss of stock value in a day, dropping $251 billion (Nix and Wagner, 2022). In the adhocracy, complacency is your greatest enemy.

Emocracy: co-creation

As we have seen by the example within Meta (Facebook), the consumer has the power to influence unlike in any other era that we have been able to document, research, or study. And this too has brought forth another source of competitive advantage. For this reason, as we are continuing onward in the post-knowledge era, there are two sources of competitive advantage that are equally dependent upon each other. And that is called co-creation. This new era of post knowledge is now being called the emocracy. It is so new that as of this writing, I cannot even find a definition through Merriam-Webster dictionary either online or abridged. But we can trace the definition back to Dr. Julian Birkinshaw (2014) through his introduction of the eras as well as in Dr. Philip Squire's (2021) continuing discourse in professionalizing sales as a chosen career pathway. In the emocracy, the consumer or buyer also has a hand in the source of competitive advantage. No longer do they have the upper hand of a meritocracy or the lower hand of a bureaucracy. They have an equal hand in the decision-making process and successful outcome from a seller as a buyer. In the emocracy part of this era, people are making more and more decisions based off their feelings, association, or recognition and internalization of goods and products and services being offered or sold to them. In short, an emocracy is where people are making decisions based off their emotions rather than factual evidence, research, or ability to make an informed decision. This is also known as the social effect of a product or service as represented in social environment, social media, and brand representation. Likewise, they are also making the same emotional appeal or identification of a need based on the organization and their employees (sales representatives) who may be their first point of contact in order to buy their products or services.

For the most part, today's modern consumers may want to know what position or stance an organization may have on such issues like politics, environment, women's rights, reproductive rights, veteran support, and how the LGBTQ members of society and employees are treated. Further, they may identify with organizations that champion multicultural generations and ethnicities, and want to know whether or not an organization supports persons with disabilities. And lately, in a heavily divided, social media radicalized world, even the support of vaccines and or mask usage and their enforcement have become major factors in deciding who to buy from or support as a consumer. This has radically changed from the previous eras and even just over the past few decades, where people made research-based, evidence-based, informed buying decisions. This is the very heart of an emocracy. For organizations to survive and evolve, they must embrace their side within the adhocracy values if they want to continue onward and thrive. For the first time in our recent documented history, both the consumer or buyer and the seller of an organization, government, or company have an equal stronghold or source of competitive advantage.

Maybe, upon reading this, you might be a bit skeptical. That is fine. Some people choose not to view the great vast world as changing and others might say emocracy is all made up. Well, let us then take a look at how even the current landscape of jobs has changed.

People are now able to get a full-time or part-time paying job and career as a social media influencer (Kirwan, 2022). "What is that?" you might ask. It is the systematic result of an emocracy, that's what it is! A social media influencer is a person who has large numbers of followers on their social media accounts. They create and post content mostly all about them or something they care about, or something they are paid to endorse. They have significant power to entice and drive their followers to look, act, behave a certain way and buy things that the social media influencer recommends or suggests. These people who function or work as social media influencers work diligently to build up their base of followers and the more people that follow them, the more trust and power they have to continue to drive others to buy whatever it is they are influencing. Imagine having that unregulated power. If you like a product or don't like a product and you are a social media influencer with massive global followers, you have the power to literally determine success or painful woes to organizations and companies. This is 100 percent real and happening today. And people buy or sell or act or react to the actions of these social media influencers. Don't believe me? Well, ask Mark Zuckerberg how he feels about losing over $250 billion because consumers are following these influencers.

Some of the highest-paid social media influencers might be some people that you have even heard of but just did not know they were also paid for influencing people's buying decisions. For example, have you ever heard of the soccer star Cristiano Ronaldo? Well, he has earned anywhere from $619,000 to $1 million per post on social media (Geyser, 2022). Or, what about Hollywood star, Dwayne "The Rock" Johnson? He has earned anywhere from $500,000 to $800,000 per post on social media. Still not convinced we are living in an emocracy where buying decisions are widely based on emotional buying and selling? Maybe you have heard of the reality television stars the Kardashians? Between Kylie Jenner and Kim Kardashian, the stars each earn between $400,000 to almost $800,000 per social media post. And this is on top of their normal jobs. And it is not just only attributed to known celebrities that are taking the roles as social media influencers. Take, for example, a 17-year-old girl named Charli

D'Amelio who has and can earn $172,700 (per post!) on Instagram (Mancilla, 2022). Yes, you read that right. And James Charles became the first male spokesperson for Covergirl in 2016 as his social media posting abilities had netted him over 20 million YouTube and 18 million Instagram followers. He is paid over $150,000 per post on social media. The list goes on and on. The role of the social media influencer is just one mainstream example of living within an emocracy. And if you as a business or organization are not holding true to adhocracy and the ability to be agile, you'll be left behind very quickly.

Where do we go from here?

As I sit and write this chapter, the world is continuing onward in both the adhocracy and the emocracy. The sources of competitive advantage are indeed depended on and driven by both the buyer and seller. And emotions are currently taking the upper hand in how products and services are sold. At this very moment, the Russian government is tragically bombing Ukraine and all of its citizens with no mercy and without following of the rules of war—whatever that means, as "rules of war" sounds like an oxymoron to me. Nevertheless, this unjust action has demonstrated the influence of emocracy. People are expressing their anger and frustrations on the actions of the Russian government by banning sales of Russian vodka across the globe. Now remember, I said earlier that in an emocracy, people are making decisions not based on fact or evidence; they are making decisions based on their feelings or emotions. This is a perfect example of how an emocracy works. People across the globe have said they are banning and destroying all Russian vodka. However, they do not know which vodka actually comes from Russia. They see a long, strange name and assume it must be Russian. Case in point: Stolichnaya Vodka, a very well-known brand, is having to change its own name from Stolichnaya to Stoli to try and distance itself from being thought of as a Russian brand (Spiegleman, 2022). Stolichnaya vodka has been produced in Latvia since 2000, not Russia. The

Smirnoff brand of vodka is in the same position. It is a British-owned product that is produced in the United States in Illinois. Yet social media and influencers drive the messaging that it is all from Russia. How do you compete as a salesperson if you are selling these brands of vodka? How do you compete as a salesperson against the powers of social media? The larger question is how do you compete with or against selling towards people's emotions? Well, the tips and tricks and overcoming objections known as consultative sales techniques of the 1980s are just no match for the adhocracy and emocracy we are living in today.

Coming back to the present-day situation, we now know the era and the sources of competitive advantage in which we are living. As I started writing this chapter, we are beginning to return to a sense of a new normal—one that is similar but already much different from that which we experienced pre-pandemic during 2019. For the most part, businesses have reopened, and people have begun to resume normal daily functions. That said, an even newer reality is happening that ties directly into the emocracy we just learnt about. This newer reality is a movement from people not wanting to go back to the way things were in 2019. People no longer want to return to the daily grind of the office routine. They have woken up to the reality of working remotely and have also experienced the benefits of being able to work more or work smarter without the need of having to commute to the cubicle world of yesteryear. A Pew Research Center polling of over 10,000 US-based employees who hold one job as their primary source of income found that nearly 61 percent of employees no longer want to return to the office to work, while 38 percent of them say they cannot return to the office due to closures or they are not permitted to return (Hoff, 2022). Again, people have evolved and have learnt how to live and work in a remote world.

So, what does this mean for salespeople, companies, and organizations in their ability to sell to individuals in this ever-changing environment? It means organizations must adapt and so must sales. The adhocracy and resisting the urge to be complacent and return to the sales processes and procedures of 2019 and earlier days will result in attracting and reaching fewer consumers. In this digital age, sales is shifting towards online. As I sit here writing, I have already had two packages delivered today of products that in 2019 I would have gone to the store and purchased. Another five packages came over the last two days. We can simply buy things online and have them delivered versus having to go and get them. And that includes the basics of groceries and staples needed for home living. What it does not mean is that sales, and sales as a profession, is dead or no longer viable. As long as we can barter and exchange goods and services globally, then sales will be viable. We simply need to adapt and ensure that we are reaching our customers in the way that they want to be sold to. Dr. Philip Squire goes into this concept of selling based on the values of how a customer wants to be sold to in greater detail and his research and advice is ever as important today if not more so for tomorrow. So, what is at the center of all of this? What two things ring loudly and clearly to you? I'll tell you. *Change* and the *individual's* right or ability to accept or reject change. People are becoming more and more awake in their understanding that change is constant, it's personal, and how they manage it will make it bearable and achievable. Those who survived the global pandemic have had their entire lives uprooted. And it continues as Europe deals with an active war between Russia and Ukraine on its doorstep. Already Iran and Israel are exchanging threats and bombs and other countries are in toxic relationships and situations. Countless millions of people are migrating from country to country trying to find a better life and the ability to live. Change is at the heart of all that we do and all that we see and I for one have never been taught by my parents, my school system, nor any elder or person on how I am supposed to manage personal change.

For the art of sales, the career path is very much alive, but we as sales professionals, old and young, must embrace change and must be able to understand what is happening not only within the organization when changes occur, but also within our customers and most importantly within ourselves. From a sales perspective, I told you earlier that with the evolution of time through the eras, and the advent of adhocracy and emocracy, that the valued tips, tricks, and how to overcome objections and how to close someone most likely will not work in today's modern sales environment. A *Forbes* article also affirmed that today's modern salesperson must adapt and work differently (Kresic, 2022). They must embrace empathy or face coming across as arrogant. In the emocracy, you are dealing with people's emotions. They no longer want to be sold to. They no longer want you to simply overcome their objection. For the most part, they might even be more educated about your product or service than you are yourself. So, for certain, do not follow an antiquated sales approach and rush to close them. The top five soft skills that are needed to facilitate today's negotiation process in an emocracy puts trust demonstrated with empathy and patience as the number one skillset. Followed by that are respectful discussions, where you share that you have the knowledge by understanding where the customer is coming from. If you think sales is a step-by-step process where you open, probe, overcome objection, and magically close, you would better serve your own interests to think about changing your mindset or possibly choosing another career pathway.

In typical sales management, the majority of thought and concern is focused on key performance indicators through the weekly numbers, advertising and marketing campaigns, and promotions in selling goods and products to a consumer. According to Bouchrika (2022), nearly $170 billion is spent in North America on training programs each year. Of that, $4.6 billion is directly related to sales training. The average company in the United States spent about $1,111 per employee on sales training and that was down $175 from 2019. So, even during the pandemic and post pandemic, companies are still heavily investing in sales training programs. But what is it that they are teaching and training their employees on? Is it the old tips, tricks, and how to overcome objections? Is it more on how to be a real person and express empathy and support humanistic emotions and behaviors? I think it is more of the same of what we have witnessed in the past. If change is constant, and we agree that a person has the right and the ability to accept or reject change—thinking of the countless millions of people refusing to return to the office right now—then do we not have a moral obligation to learn how to manage personal change and support our sales teams and greater employees through change? I say that more than ever, it is our respon-sibility as sales leaders and supervisors to embrace the adhocracy and emocracy and learn this valuable skillset. We can no longer afford to be complacent. Just ask Mark Zuckerberg. There is a cost to compla-cency and we can no longer ignore that people have a right to accept or reject change in the emocracy. Just ask the millions of people who have said no to the return to office demand. In this next chapter, I will share why I feel this transition and focus on personal change is so important and how I came up with the new model for managing personal change called SCARED SO WHAT.

04

Focusing on individuals

Within sales, the people we have on our teams are our greatest asset and opportunity to achieve our sales goals and deliver our mission in becoming and remaining profitable. It is astonishing to me how a few organizations treat their salesforce as machines or order takers and continuously drive them to do anything and everything to achieve the company goals without regard for their personal wellbeing. I would like to believe that this is not the norm and I know that, in the majority, there are wonderful organizations that do believe in and treat their sales team members as their greatest asset. I know for certain the company that I work for does just that and I'm hopeful your experience is the same. Salespeople are the front line and will be the receivers of the full blunt force of change and counter actions of what the internal organization demands of them. Those that do not focus on their salesforce as the human beings they are, and value them immensely as their greatest asset, are morally inept in my viewpoint. Change has real consequences. Being a part of sales leadership means that we are entrusted to lead our own members in our care through change. And that is not easy to do if the leaders do not invest in learning the skillsets and competencies it takes to lead in this way.

This is where we get into the discussion of leadership styles and how to lead as a sales supervisor or leader. So, let's discuss the concept of leadership as a transaction. Leading transactionally means that you are ticking all of the boxes and ensuring that a team is achieving all of the necessary tasks and opportunities that we come across each day of the year. But leading transformationally (*Leading Sales Transformation*) means that, as a leader, you must put forward the responsibility and care of those you are entrusted to lead. And this means that you must consider each of them as individuals and foster their own sense of development and personal growth, generate and facilitate learning opportunities, and yes, help them in managing personal change. To transform is to change permanently and not go back to the way things were before. Leading that change process as a sales leader requires that you need to expand your own knowledge of what it means to lead change and know that for the individual involved it is almost always personal. It is imperative that you know that there is a difference in leadership styles and practices. As such, we have the opportunity to set ourselves apart by learning how to lead others through change if we truly want to transform our organization and our people. So, that raises the question surrounding the root of personal change.

There is a clinical term known as *metathesiophobia*, which is the official term for the fear of change. It is real and can paralyze people who have this condition. But for countless others and the vast majority of people we may work with and know, it manifests itself in many different ways. Regardless of whether the change scenario is positive or negative, we may still feel anxiety, stress, or a sense of loss of comfort. To understand this further, reflect with me for a little bit and see if you agree.

Think of a positive change scenario like getting married, buying a new car, getting your driver's license, moving to a new town, or exceeding your sales goals for the quarter. All these actions could be considered positive. However, you still may feel anxiety, be nervous, feel stress, and question if you are doing the right thing in the moment or be traumatized with the thought of what is next. You may feel a rush of breath or racing heartbeat; you might even get goosebumps when thinking about what surpassing a sales goal might mean for you. Your body experiences nearly the same reactions to a positive change as you may experience in a negative change. In essence, you do not have to be scared of change to feel all its effects.

Throughout my research many people asked me right off the bat, "Why do you feel the need to create another change model?" My initial internal reaction always harks back to the personal change piece of it.

Stop for a moment and reflect back to a time when you were young. Did your mom or dad or perhaps your grandparents, aunts, or uncles, or maybe your teachers ever say to you, "Don't worry about it"? Perhaps they may have said something along the lines of, "You're gonna be fine. You're worrying for nothing." Or maybe they said things like, "Grow up," "Be a man," "Don't let them see you sweat." Or maybe, worse yet, they said, "There's nothing you can do about it." We've all heard those things from people around us. But I ask you, have these words ever led to sweet relief? Did these words ever make you feel better? More often than not, the answer is no. They don't make us feel any better. But why is that? Why do we not learn how to manage personal change?

The reason these words, even when offered in care, often do not work is because our body and brain are telling us that something is wrong or off. The best these people, our parents and others, can give us is to offer kind words or phrases as an unintended guide to simply "brush it off." The truth of the matter is that they do not know how to manage personal change for themselves. What makes us think that they will be able to help us in managing our own instance of personal change? At some point, we all have to learn how. When I share this illustration with others, they immediately get it and understand the need to learn how to manage personal change for themselves and also to support others.

People also ask me why I am concerned about individuals' involvement or understanding about personal change. As much as I intended for my research to yield critical reviews of the major change models that exist today, my search for personal change models pulled me into the broad spectrum of organizational and developmental change management with a strong focus on business needs. The focus, I have found, is almost entirely embedded and deeply rooted into change management to drive organizational change. The focus was not generally concerned with the persons involved and their own personal change, but more so on how to execute and facilitate change for organizations at large. In his review, "Change management models: A comparative analysis and concerns," Joseph Galli (2018) said, "Change is inevitable, whether it is personal or professional." Creasy

(2018) stated that change management, also known as "CM," is "the application of a structured process and set of tools for leading the people side of change to achieve a desired business outcome."

Rune Todnem (2005), in his work titled "Organizational change management: A critical review," cited Balogun and Hope Hailey's (2004) comment that "the management of organizational change currently tends to be reactive... ad hoc, with a reported failure rate of around 70 per cent of all change programmes initiated."

These statements concerned me greatly in the fact that if one follows the key words they reference, we will see their focus was almost entirely on organizational/developmental change for the company; they did not focus on the person that needs to execute the change. The words "business outcome," "management," and "organization" were the key words directing their focus. How is a person required to execute change when we are not focusing on their personal change needs? The people themselves need to buy into the change, accept it, reject it, and understand what their part and role will be to execute it. I believed we were missing that piece, which may contribute to why people consistently reference that up to 70 percent (Balogun and Hope Hailey, 2004) of change programs fail.

What were my research aims?

My aim was to understand if my new model, SCARED SO WHAT (Van Ulbrich, 2020), could be useful and effective to support the individual in understanding and navigating personal change, either at work, or for personal and situational use outside of work. I did this by disseminating the model to our employees and to others externally for test and review. As Grant (2014) references, "The more you give, the more you want to do it – as do others around you." Kurt Lewin also states that "People support what they create" (Graban and Swartz, 2013). These are key ingredients as I wanted to give the models to others, thus allowing them to support the creation and evolution of the SCARED SO WHAT model. My main objectives in doing this research were to:

- engage my global sales employee base in reviewing the model for usefulness and gain their feedback
- review the model for usefulness by introducing it externally to my travel customer base to gain their feedback
- collect data responses both quantitative and qualitative to assess feasibility and usefulness and or to change and adapt the model
- package the model into a user-friendly digestible presentation
- get the model published in a professional journal for further peer and academic feedback and further the discussion.

By performing these objectives, I was able to assess feedback and incorporate it into my scholarly work and gain valuable insight into the usefulness of the model. In leading change, a leader creates the vision and strategy for the team to manage and create plans and actions to achieve the end goal (Kotter, 2012).

My focus for the SCARED SO WHAT model is towards the individual as a self-discovery methodology. That is the main idea in creating the model. But my research also supports that the model can be easily utilized as a coaching tool, whereby each section becomes a stage or focal point, allowing the coach to ask open-ended questions of the coachee and guide them through the process towards managing change. The SCARED portion helps us reflect on the change we are experiencing so we can make a favorable decision. We are still left asking, "So what does it mean?" or "So what can we do about it?," which is where the SO WHAT portion of the model comes into play. However, the SCARED portion of the model is designed as a way for us to critically reflect for ourselves and walk our own way through a personal change situation. No longer do we have to ask someone else to help calm us down or help us decide— we can think it through ourselves or include others on our own reflective journey.

Why is the individual the most important element in change management and overall success in sales?

As sales leaders it is imperative for us to consider other alternative models like SCARED SO WHAT if we are going to be able to critically support our salespeople. We cannot simply use the same models for each and every change scenario. Schech-Storz (2013) surmises that, "not all changes are the same; therefore, management needs to use different change models and methodologies depending on the situation." And deep down we know this to be true. At this very moment, sales leaders reading this book should be asking themselves, what do I do to support my sales team through change? What do we have within our organization to help people through change as individuals? Perhaps you have used some of the organizational change models we have uncovered within this reading. That would be great. But are they designed to incorporate the individual's own needs, or the needs of the organization? Think on that for a moment. The answers just might scare you. Because what you find may not be suitable for individual change management or you may not find anything at all.

The individual journey through change is the most critical element within an organization. Galli (2018), Mulholland (2021), and Todnem (2005) all reference that change will most definitely fail if the individual is not made the primary focus. Van De Ven and Sun (2017) critically review the breakdowns of change and state, saying, "Change agents typically respond to these breakdowns by taking actions to 'CORRECT' people... so they 'CONFORM' to their model of change." That right there says all I need to know and tells me that focusing on my salespeople's own individual needs will further garnish a successful outcome not only for an organization but for the individuals themselves. And that is leading transformationally by thinking of the salespeople's needs as well as the needs of the organization when it comes to managing change.

When reflecting on why salespeople are the critical element in change management and our ultimate success, I first look directly at the salespeople that I am in charge of. A major function of my role is to support their overall development, their growth, and supply them with the knowledge of sales from a science and psychology-based practice. The salesperson is the key to our overall success, and it is the salesperson that has to experience the effects of change and yet still find a way to negotiate and make the sale. Organizational change models are very helpful and important for what they are designed to achieve. But in my view, the individual expected to carry out the change deserves to have a mechanism of support to facilitate their own understanding of change that is happening not only around them, but to them as well. Their mental and physical wellbeing can determine the outcomes for the entire organization.

A salesperson goes through constant situations and incidents of change, whether imposed upon them through their employer or through the actions or inactions of their clients and customers they serve each day. Think about the salesperson's main role. It is to negotiate and facilitate deal making to support the customer's wants and needs while also supporting the revenue generation between a customer and their employer. That employer could even be themselves if they are self-employed. Situations with negotiation, objections to the products or services offered by the salesperson, to outright rejection of those products and services or even the salesperson themselves. The role of a salesperson is constant action and reaction in facilitating a sales process that will generate a result in a successful outcome for all involved. Whenever one door closes, the salesperson must embrace the impact of that change situation and it is personal. Salespeople put a lot of energy into planning, supporting, prospecting, researching, and communicating between the organization and potential and current customers. They are the go-between in most cases between the organization and the consumer. And often, that leads to countless bouts of rejected sales pitches, proposals, and deals for every single positive sale. Many people in sales facilitate rejection the same way anyone else would—negatively. It can be a frightening experience if or when targets and goals are not achieved. Likewise, if large sales actions result in favorable outcomes, many salespeople want to stop to enjoy that exciting situation. If proper recognition and reward is not encountered or supported by the organization, this can also lead to a negative change situation for the seller. This happens more often than not, simply because the organization moves on and says, "Give us more and do it now."

Knowing that salespeople will either accept or reject change at an individual level, a CM model needs to focus on individuals. Within the model I created, I set out to create a support model that would promote critical reflection in the face of change. At the core of the model is the users' ability to choose and recognize their own feelings instead of prescribing the outcome as many organizational change models do.

I believe a person has the right to choose if they want to accept or reject personal change, and this is where the other models fell short (in large part due to the fact that they weren't created specifically with sales professionals in mind!). A person can become stuck within a change situation and not know where they stand regarding the change. Likewise, others may be completely indifferent to the change situation they are experiencing. People are complex and therefore any change model to focus on the individual needs to be flexible and inclusive of the human needs and ability to choose. Salespeople are no different from others, but by the very nature of their career pathway and the consistent levels of change they succumb to because of their job, for them to be even more successful, they need to learn how to embrace their own bouts of personal change. SCARED SO WHAT allows for that personal choice to happen based on positive, neutral, and negative energy levels of change. And further, it can help them in navigating their own way during a personal change situation by using critical reflection.

How do I know if SCARED SO WHAT can work?

By October 2019, I had already completed module three of the master's program with Consalia (2019) and had begun module four on Leading Collaborative Change. Simultaneously, at my organization, in my role of leading sales transformation for the international sales teams, I had just completed launching the first learning pathway in our new digital sales training program. This new sales education program was the first version of a sales manual and represented how they were to perform in their sales role. It was 100 percent digital, portable, and mobile for them to learn anywhere they desired. It would focus on the actions necessary for the salesperson to achieve on a consistent basis to generate results. And it would provide the salesperson with the resources and generate the knowledge necessary for them to be successful within the organization. The master's program and Consalia were helping me to shape the sales training of the future for my sales teams in Europe, the Middle East, and Africa, and soon to other global regions.

Whilst continuing onward within the master's program and my daily work, I noticed that the adoption rate and utilization of the digital sales academy was not happening with the speed and acceptance that I had anticipated. "Why are the teams not using the program?" was a question I pondered night and day, and so did my supervisor. Bassot's (2016) teaching on reflection in and on action were helping me to uncover this mystery as I was continuing to think and reflect on my actions taken to lead the teams. It would only be through module four of the master's, on Leading Collaborative Change, that I would be able to uncover the possible answer to my question.

As I shared earlier, during module four, we focused heavily on change and the causes and effects with variable change models. My "ah ha" moment came during those classes. Brown, Heyer, and Ettenson (2013) articulated it best by stating, "Not being able to articulate why the project is being done, puts it at risk of losing support and momentum and decreases its chance of success." I readily identified with that statement in the fact I failed to explain why our sales leaders needed to launch the sales academy program for and with their teams during that time. By the same token, I did not take into consideration the understanding or the needs of the individual team members who were to participate in the digital program. It was so obvious to me that the program was necessary, but my launch plan did not include the needs of the individual nor their ability to understand why the change needed to occur. In failing to explain the why, they went on as normal with the attitude of "we'll get to it when we get to it." I had later confirmed this by speaking with each of the leaders and multiple team members.

Suspecting why it failed, I was left searching for a way to explain the change process and bring them along on the journey. I was very conflicted with the change models we learnt about. As I stated earlier, to me, they all appeared prescriptive towards a negative change action and not providing personal choice or ability to fluctuate between negative and positive energy. What happens if the change is a good thing? What happens if I'm indifferent to the change? What happens if I reject the change? These were questions I began to ask myself. I needed to recognize that the sales employees were experiencing change and I was the instigator of that change by introducing a new sales academy for them to participate in. I could have used any one of the organizational change models *on* them. But I knew already that they would not address their own personal reflection on this change. Therefore, I decided to use SCARED SO WHAT as a way of talking with them about the change scenario of participating in the new sales academy. I needed to introduce them to learn a new way of managing their own feelings and actions towards change.

I created a new digital pathway called managing personal change with SCARED SO WHAT within our company's learning and management system. It was brief, easy to participate and view, and included a mix of digital text and video content. The whole learning brief took about 30 minutes of their time. I then conveyed the importance of my task in teaching them how to learn to manage personal change for themselves with their supervisors around the global markets within my care. And then I introduced the online module to the sales members and gave them a timeline of when they had to complete it. It was also the beginning of the pandemic and fear was rife throughout the organization as well as with our travel agency customers. Little did I know that this would be the perfect fear-engaging storm to learn if the new model would work or not.

As our cruise industry was grinding to a complete halt, the same was happening with our travel agency customers. But our team had taken the SCARED SO WHAT digital learning pathway and continued to further their skillsets in learning how to navigate personal change. A surprise was that they were not only using it for themselves, but they were using it for and with our travel agency customers as well. Salespeople within and outside our organization were learning to manage their own fearful situations in dealing with work and their personal lives during the early stages of the pandemic. Our sales team members were appearing to present themselves in a stronger, more confident position and facilitating the needs to support our travel customers as well. Often, I would hear sales members referring to SCARED SO WHAT. We took the sharing of the model a step further and presented the digital training course to our travel agency customers throughout Europe, the Middle East, and Africa. I had travel agents emailing and talking with their sales representatives and myself saying they were utilizing the model not only with their fellow agents, but with their families and children as well. The model was filling that gap of understanding how to manage personal change.

Throughout the pandemic, while other organizations were streamlining and shutting down their sales teams within the cruise industry, my organization kept ours strong. We did make some adjustments and lost a few, but overall, we maintained a very strong presence within all of our markets to support our travel agency customers. We also decided that this was the right time to relaunch our sales academy as we had the time to invest in ourselves while we waited out the pandemic until we could get our fleets back up and sailing with customers. And this time, the sales team members were reminded about the SCARED SO WHAT methodology first before they decided to participate in the sales academy. We focused on them and their needs and understanding first, and the model, as stated by them, helped them facilitate their own decision-making towards positive development. The uptake in the sales academy was extremely favorable this time around.

Why might change management and organizational change models not be the best fit for individuals?

I do not believe that one model can facilitate all aspects of change, whether it be for an organization or an individual. As I have illustrated through my research, there are many very influential change models in use in the world today. However, the majority of those change models are focused on the organization's needs and not necessarily the needs of the individual—as evidenced by their own write-up and accreditation. Often, I am found within a conversation about why I created the new personal change model with other leaders outside of my industry. I posit this managerial situation to them: "If you are leading sales members, regardless of where, how many, their cultural differences, nuances, etc., and you implement change within your team and organization, wouldn't you want to know who the change adaptors and change detractors are? Would you not want to know if someone accepts the changes you are imposing on them? Furthermore, would you want to recruit those change adaptors to help facilitate your changes? And if you find that you have change detractors on your team, wouldn't you want to be able to try and coach them towards a different outcome that could be successful for them as well as the organization?" When I begin to share these types of questions with other leaders, they then can see how the other models might not be able to facilitate that level of questioning and understanding. I further ask, are we leading transactionally, or should we be leading in a transformational way that includes the individual's own further development? I prefer the latter. And to do that, I believe we need to include the individual's own needs within the change needs of the organization.

My creation of the new personal change model and my research in no way posits that the existing change models in the world today are not relevant. On the contrary, they are very relevant. In my discussions with those tasked with facilitating and leading change within our own organization and externally, what comes back is that there can be a combination. And for this, I agree. I created SCARED SO WHAT for my own use to help my sales team learn how to embrace and manage the personal change they experience each and every day in their career as a salesperson. But I also have discovered that whenever we are launching a change initiative within our organization, we can use one or a combination of several organizational change models to facilitate the organizational change required. But at the same time, once we explain the change needed to the sales members, we can then use SCARED SO WHAT for them to facilitate their own sense of understanding about the change as it impacts them. As a leader, I can even use SCARED SO WHAT as a coaching mechanism to find out where the sales members are during the change. Simply by asking open-ended questions using the stages of the model, we can guide each other towards a decision. Once a decision has been made, then we can work together on creating a SO WHAT plan to action the change for the individual and use an organizational model to implement within the organization. For me, this facilitates everyone involved in executing and facilitating a change process. The organization, the individuals, and supervisors are required to implement the change process all together.

As I have illustrated several times, change is constant, and we can always expect more. But change is also personal. Therefore, how you manage it makes it bearable and achievable. The next time you go to implement a change with your sales team—or any team or on anyone – think to yourself, am I including the individual's own needs or concern on this change journey regardless of if I think it is a positive or negative change? If the answer is no, then perhaps consider learning more about SCARED SO WHAT and why it is important. In the next chapter, that is exactly what we will do.

05

The personal change management model: SCARED SO WHAT

This chapter explains what types of personal change this model can be used for. At the end of the chapter I will explain how it has been used to date.

SCARED SO WHAT was created in the scarcity of a relative model or methodology to help the individual to navigate their own way through personal change. This is not an organizational change model, but it can be used by sales leaders and organizations to support their individuals' own understanding of how change affects them. I designed and researched this new model as part of my master's in Leading Sales Transformation with Consalia Sales Business School and Middlesex University of London from 2018 to 2020. In doing so, I put this model into practice within my sales organization as a way to help the sales members learn how to embrace the challenges through change that they experience each day in their chosen sales profession. As a result of sharing the model with our internal sales members, the climate was unfortunately ripe with change due to the oncoming global pandemic known as Covid-19. The opportunity to challenge the validity of the SCARED SO WHAT model was a case of being in the right moment and the right time. Not only were my sales members experiencing this significant bout of global change, but so were our customers and their friends, family members, and colleagues as well. SCARED SO WHAT made its way beyond our sales team to other members within our organization as well as to our B2B travel agency customers and beyond through their professional and personal networks. The program continued to expand beyond my intended reach when it was published in the *International Journal of Sales Transformation* (Van Ulbrich, 2020a) along with the *Change Management Review* (Van Ulbrich, 2020b). Additionally, I have published the model itself for all persons around the globe who have access to the internet to be able to freely download and absorb for themselves (Van Ulbrich, 2020c). This was critically important to me because of my strong belief that we could support this current generation and future ones as well to navigate their lives with greater understanding and ease if they can only learn how to manage their own bouts of personal change. Imagine the outcomes. This is something I do every day. Let us now take a look at what the SCARED SO WHAT methodology for navigating personal change is all about.

First and foremost, this model is unique in its individualistic design because it provides a roadmap for the ultimate questions someone may have after they have made a decision about a situation. The questions that an individual has after making a decision about a personal change situation typically are either "SO WHAT can I do about it?" or "SO WHAT does it mean to me?" As a result, SCARED SO WHAT is two models in one, which if used together create a methodology or framework for navigating personal change. Let us now look at the first part called SCARED.

The SCARED Wheel of Change

SCARED is the first part of this change framework and it is represented by a wheel to facilitate understanding about individual change. A key point to know is that you do not have to literally be scared to use this framework of reflection and action. While the fear of change is called *metathesiophobia*, people with this deep fear may readily be able to identify with the model. For most people, change can be scary. However, change can also be positive as I have described earlier, with examples such as buying a new home, getting married, buying a new car, getting a part in a school play, or the leading position or role on a team. Regardless of if the change is positive or negative, you do not have to take the word SCARED literally to be able to benefit from using it. Over one's lifespan, people will have different reactions to change. People can experience energy reactions to change such as neutral, positive, or negative reactions in their behavior as each element applies to them in their current situation. I have designed SCARED based on those energy levels. And at the heart of this reflective model is *you*, the individual, and the change you are experiencing. Together, you are one and the same (see Figure 5.1).

Before I go too far in explaining what the SCARED model means, I want to share with you a lesson that I learnt from Ken Ross, the son of Dr. Elisabeth Kübler-Ross, creator of the 5 Stages of Grief®, also known as the Change Curve, which I value and respect immensely along with the other models I shared with you earlier. In my interview with him,[1] Ken informed me that his mother was criticized by both the medical profession as well as individuals outside of medicine, stating that her model was linear and was to be used in a linear fashion. She would say that was not true and that was not how she designed it. "She just wanted to facilitate a conversation," Ken said. And with that lesson learnt, it is important that I also

FIGURE 5.1 The SCARED Wheel of Change

share with you that the SCARED SO WHAT model is *not* a linear model either. Like Dr. Kübler-Ross, I too am trying to help you facilitate a conversation. A conversation with yourself or with others in critical reflection. My goal is for you to stop and learn how to critically reflect on a personal change situation you experience. During that situation, much like the way we learn is very scattered, you can bounce back and forth, in-between, or skip some points altogether. So do not think that you have to go in any specific order, because you do not. This is a way for you to not be afraid or stress over change, but to stop and think it through.

Knowing that you are at the center of the model and synonymous with the personal change situation you are experiencing, the first energy element you may encounter is *Surprise.* This element of change can be expected, unexpected, imposed, or not evoking any form of an emotional reaction from you. That is why change is personal. It affects you individually and you alone will determine how you react to change that affects you. Surprise can be measured in response to a change on all three energy levels. You could be pleasantly surprised by the change. Likewise, you could be neutral and not really affected by the change. And the opposite of positive, you could be negatively surprised by the change you experience. The first element of understanding the SCARED process is to identify how the change is affecting you based on these three energy categories. This is the first part of critical reflection. Instead of just worrying about it, you are stopping and reflecting on the change that you are involved with and asking yourself these guidance points as questions: "Am I surprised by this change?" Then reflect if it is positive, neutral, or negative as a benchmark.

The next feeling or action point might be to ask yourself, "Do I *Champion* this change or am I *Conflicted* by it? Or does it affect me at all?" Let us first focus on the positive energy side with Champion. If you can say that you champion the change, this means to you that you are ok with it. You may be very excited about the change, or you may just think, "Eh... This is kind of ok! I can support this."

Champion represents a positive reaction to the change and is measured favorably. In the middle, there is still the element of neutrality.

Maybe you are not sure of the effects of this change just yet. So, you might be in a neutral state of emotion waiting for further information or actions to reveal themselves to you. But what if you are not happy with the change? Then as this most likely is your first absorption to the change and you are feeling negative about it, it can be represented by the word conflicted, which means you have a conflict with this change. You are not agreeing to it at this stage. And it is important to know that it is ok to feel negative about a change situation. Not every change is positive, but if we think it through a little bit, we might be able to find something positive about it. And then again, we might not. Again, change is personal.

Now that you are starting to reflect on the change that you are experiencing, we can move onto the next item that most typically can help to influence any change outcome. *Actions* are at the heart of understanding most anything in the world today. Within communication, what actions will you take to bring forth more information to help you facilitate understanding? In essence, what are you going to do to understand the change you are experiencing? Actions can be simple or very complex depending on what you are feeling. An action could be asking a friend, boss, colleague or team member, mom or dad, aunt or uncle, or anyone for that matter, a question. The act of simply asking questions is an action. With that action a reaction should occur and help to generate further evidence or awareness of the situation or subject you are inquiring about. This helps to facilitate understanding. That is the entire reason why we ask questions in the first place. To facilitate meaning and understanding and further our knowledge. Maybe you need to send an email, call a friend, perform some research—either way, you are asking for information. Now most of the times, people experience change and start to worry and fester over change—especially when it is negative. What I am saying for you to do here is to continue your act of critical reflection before you make any decision about the change. Perform an action or multiple actions to gain a better understanding of what the change means to you. At this point, you are not trying to make a decision, but rather you are gathering evidence to support you making an informed decision. That is a very big difference in the way most people navigate change today. You probably have heard of people making a "knee-jerk decision" or "instant decision." Those terms reference someone who did not put any sincere thought into making their decision. Others might say they have made an uninformed decision. This happens a lot in today's emocracy where people are making decisions based on emotions rather than factual evidence. Actions are a part of critical reflection and can be your best source of seeking out information.

Have you ever heard the phrase "the action is where it's at?" That's because it is what we do through actions that keep us informed. Guessing or assuming is the lazy way out and does not lead to formulating an informed decision.

If you are now starting to reflect on how you feel during a change situation, you may have already assessed your level of surprise to it. And you might have already thought about how you feel towards the change in reference to whether you champion it or if you are conflicted by it. From there, you could now begin taking actions to bring in further information about the change to help facilitate your understanding of the situation you are experiencing. By taking actions, you are now either unconsciously or sometimes consciously shaping your reactions to the change. And this brings us to the next element on the SCARED Wheel of Change model. That is represented with *Receptive* or *Rejective*. At some point you will encounter one of these energy elements, and you may be neutral to the change as well. Receptive represents the positive energy side. You might find yourself saying, "I'm ok with this" or "I like this" and that could represent that you are more receptive of your personal change situation. Likewise, you could be barely affected by this change event and could find yourself in a neutral state. But more often than not, you would find yourself leaning one way or the other. At the negative energy side is rejective. This means that you are not comfortable with the change and are rejecting that it is happening to you or with you. That is fine. It is a perfectly normal way to react to change. Not every change situation that happens to us or is imposed upon us are we magically going to accept. That was at the very heart of why I created this new model. People can reject change outright. In sales

THE PERSONAL CHANGE MANAGEMENT MODEL: SCARED SO WHAT   99

and business, a person who rejects organizational change might be known as a "change detractor." That simply means that you are not in agreement with the organization's decision to impose this change. At this stage, that is still fine, because if you remain true to yourself and give yourself the opportunity to continue reflecting on the change, you may very well come up with a different direction. Regardless of whether you are receptive or rejective within your own personal change situation, you still will ask, "So what now?" or "So, what does it mean?" or "So what can I do about it?" But don't stop yet, you are not finished with your own critical reflection. You want to make the best-informed decision you can, so continue onward and give yourself the proper chance.

Not every person will be honest within a change situation to themselves. And that means that not everyone will take the actions necessary to stop, reflect, and understand the change that is happening to them or with them. That is where those knee-jerk, rapid, assuming decisions can be made. Since actions are so critically important to bring in and understand, the next energy element is *Explore* and this is another action chance to explore other opportunities before you make a final decision about the change. You may be leaning one way or the other, either more receptive or more rejective... and you may also just not know what to do about your change situation. Explore other options is a second chance to formulate actions. What other options or opportunities are there because of this change you are in? If you are leaning towards being receptive, great! Then move forward. But if you are leaning towards rejecting the change, could you give yourself that one extra opportunity to find further information? Yes, you can if you want to. And you may or may not make a different decision. But at least you can say you have made an informed decision.

And that brings us to the last stage of the SCARED model. *Decision* or *Indecision* might be the final outcomes of your critical reflection on the change situation you are experiencing. Decision can be measured on all three energy levels. You can be positive and make a favorable decision towards the change. You can be neutral about it and the change really might not affect you that much, so you decide to just go along with it. But one can also make a negative decision about the change and reject it all together. After all, we are human. Just because we have found ourselves in a change situation does not mean we have to accept it or join in. A negative decision not to accept or participate in the change may be the right answer for you at this moment and time. Only you can make that decision. But again, if you decide that the change is not for you, you might find yourself asking, "So what now? What do I do?"

Regardless of whether you have made a favorable or unfavorable decision about your change situation, the decision is yours to make. But you want to be able to say that you made an informed decision. You want to give yourself the benefit of doubt and try to critically reflect on how the change is affecting you. Remember back when I shared with you that for me as a child... and even as an adult... people might say, "Don't worry about it," or "Don't be scared," or "It will all be fine—stop worrying." None of those things made me feel good about the change I was experiencing. Using SCARED and critically reflecting and generating actions to help me understand how this change affects me can alleviate those worries, stresses, and anxieties, and help that fear subside. The model can help me to navigate my own way through understanding my feelings towards change.

Now let me ask you this: have you ever been in a change situation where you find that you cannot make a decision, either favorable or unfavorable? Sometimes you find yourself saying, "I don't know." Another way to describe this is indecision. It means that you cannot make up your mind. In this situation, more often than not, you probably could do more actions or explore further options to gain information to help you make an informed decision either way. Remember, action is where it is all at! Actions produce information or data. These data points are bits of information for you to help process how you feel about a change scenario. If you find yourself in indecision, try to facilitate some or more actions and explore further options or opportunities. That may mean that you would want to involve others to help you make an informed decision by seeking their guidance and advice or even asking them to coach you on your situation. And this is the goal that you are looking for in using the

SCARED model as a mode of critical reflection on a change situation. Your goal is to make an informed decision that is right for you. And that means it could be favorable or unfavorable. Your decision will have consequences, but at least you can say you have thought it over diligently and you are making the best possible decision for your own situation.

This is a lot of information for some to take in. Perhaps this might be the first time you have thought about personal change and what it means to your sales team members. That is completely fine. The very fact that you are reading this far in means that you are committed to your team members and care about their own development and understanding. I praise you for that! While it may seem tedious at this moment, I assure you that once you understand how the model is intended to work, you will find it very easy to wield in your daily practice in leading your sales teams through transformation.

But isn't the model to be used in a linear way?

This is an important question. And even though I have already answered it earlier, it is worth exploring WHY it is not a linear model. First let me relate this back to how people learn. Most people think that learning is a linear function and that once the information comes in, that learning is facilitated and thus knowledge is generated. We are all instantly enlightened. Unfortunately, that is not true. As Guy Claxton (2006) iterates, the process of learning is not linear and often leads to a learning fog. We do not simply read, listen to a lecture, take a class, and magically learn. Within our minds, we bounce information back and forth between awareness and cognitive receptors. Learning is a messy process that involves many different elements: reading, writing, comprehension, questioning, testing the theory, trying out actions, all while facilitating elements of generating knowledge or awareness of understanding. This is important to realize and understand because utilizing the SCARED model in a linear fashion does not represent how people learn. Looking at Figure 5.2 you can begin to understand how the model is flexible and can bounce back

FIGURE 5.2 SCARED over time and energy

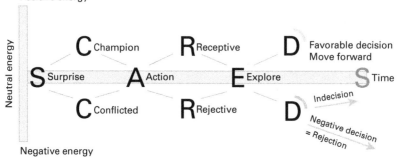

Personal Change over time. No stage is fixed. Not linear. Moves up and down as you move.

and forth between positive, neutral, and negative energy. Through actions and exploring options and opportunities, we generate bits of information that when analyzed through critical reflection, enable us to work towards making an informed learnt decision. But it is not easy. We might find our way towards making an informed favorable decision. If so, then we can continue onward to begin formulating our own SO WHAT plan. But oftentimes, people might get caught up in indecision. At that stage, there is more learning to be achieved and they might find themselves going through the model at various stages again. They can facilitate this by going back and focusing on further actions or exploring additional options to continue the learning journey about the change situation they are in.

Also, at the negative side of embracing change is another term we have discussed called rejection. This means that a person has made a negative decision, hopefully an informed one, where they have exercised actions and explored further options or opportunities, but in the end decided that this change just is not right for them. And that is fine. Change is personal and not every change is for everyone. But as you see the lines that interconnect each thought aspect on the energy levels, depending on your own personal feelings and situation towards the change you are experiencing, these letters as plots on a grid will move up and down. Sometimes people will go back and revisit elements, others may skip an element. So, the process is not linear at all but rather much like the way we learn. It's a bit messy. Feelings can be messy sometimes and that is why I created the SCARED model to help us stop, critically reflect on those feelings, and break down the change situation we are in. I did this so that we can try and bring actions and opportunities to learn more about the change happening so that we can make an informed decision, rather than an assumption or guesstimate. In the next chapter, I will take you through how you can use the SCARED model to support your sales members through personal change. This is critical to their success, as we have not been taught how to deal with personal change—change that comes from mounting pressures to sell and reach targets, to facing rejection in a sales pitch or negotiation, to dealing with familial issues and bringing them to work, and so much more. And as a leader leading your sales members, wouldn't you want to give them everything you can to help them navigate their way through change if it meant helping them to be more successful? Of course you would. That is being a transformational leader! But first, we need to explore the other side of the model – the SO WHAT element.

Great! I've made an informed decision. So, what now?

We have uncovered that the majority of CM models are to be used by the organizations themselves. Obviously, there are exceptions (Kübler-Ross' model, ADKAR, and the Conner models) that do include some elements of the individual. Kübler-Ross' model for certain as it is about the individual's own acceptance of death and dying. But for the most part, the organization is using one or more of these models in order to facilitate a change in process, structure, or way of working. Often, these models are used *on* you rather that with you or for you. And somehow at the end stage, everyone will magically accept the change. I find that very interesting, especially when there is evidence to the contrary, which is why so much literature states that change management processes have a higher tendency for failure—as we have talked about in earlier chapters. The one thing that most scholars and change leaders will agree upon is that for change to be successful, focus needs to be on the individual.

So what does one do after they have made a decision? What makes SO WHAT so different from the other models? The key answer here is this: SO WHAT is the act of making your own strategic plan in facilitating your own change. In business, we often create strategy plans. We have annual planning sessions where we get everyone together to find out what we are going to do and how we are going to do it for each quarter and for the year. That is on the large scale. In everyday work and the sales process, we also have strategy sessions where we work with each other to find out how we are going to achieve actions to generate success. SO WHAT is the process of creating your own personal strategy plan for actioning the change you have made an informed decision about. Here is how it works.

In Figure 5.3, we can see the SO WHAT Wheel to Navigate Change, which is designed to help someone create their own strategy plan for their individual change situation.

This portion of the model is much like the SCARED portion. It is not linear either, but you do start off with the first two parts together and then you may bounce around a bit. The goal is to break out and finish your change process by taking full ownership of your own

FIGURE 5.3 SO WHAT Wheel to Navigate Change

change situation. You will notice the similarity in the fact that *you* are at the center of the change. You are synonymous with the change itself. This is your own SO WHAT plan on how you will take your change situation forward.

As I mentioned earlier, we can relate to a good strategy plan in a business setting. So why is it that we cannot do the same for ourselves either within a business setting or a personal setting at home or with others? The answer is, we can. But we have not been taught to think about personal change in that way. We have been told to "not worry, just deal with it, it will all work out by itself." And we should know better. If we want something done right, then we need to take ownership for our own actions. Change doesn't have to be any different. Once we have made an informed decision, it is time for us to start thinking about what our strategy is. *Strategy* is the first step. Here is where you want to look at all the options and steps you can take to ensure your strategy for either accepting or rejecting this change decision you have made is supported in the way you desire.

When you focus on building your strategy it does not have to be very complicated. The simpler you make it, the more realistic your chance for a successful outcome. In developing your own strategy, you want to think of things to include such as:

Strategy

- Identify and clarify what the change itself is. What is the issue and your key objectives?
- Identify the steps to include in the change process. What is it that you need to do?
- Identify what processes and what people need to be involved in executing the change.
- Identify your own needs. What constraints might you have? What support mechanisms are there for you to rely on? Is a budget involved? Are there tools that can support you?
- Identify what your timeline is for this change. What and by when do things need to happen?

Likewise, as in business, when people are creating strategic plans no matter the size and scope, people always want to look at all the options and opportunities that are available to them to support the strategic planning process. Individuals are the same; we can be strategic in the way we align our thinking and should do the same to support ourselves in navigating through personal change. When it comes to *Options* or *Opportunities*, you might want to consider the following:

Options

- Have you identified other options or opportunities to support your strategic plan?
- Can you socialize your SO WHAT plan with others to gain feedback and support?
- For those people, processes that are necessary to support your strategic plan, can you fact check and gain a sense of reassurance that they are the right people to support you?
- Could you conduct a small brainstorming session or workshop for idea generation?
- What other support might be needed? Who else needs to know or be aware?

The key in building a solid personal strategy plan is to ensure that you think it through. Look at all the options and opportunities that are available to support you in being successful with your personal change decision. Once you have achieved this then you can move forward where there are two sense checks for you to stop and critically reflect on. The first one of those sense checks is finding your *Way forward*. Here in this portion of the model you want to consider the following:

Way forward

- Have I identified who will need to be in the review or support process if necessary? That is, who do I need to check with to ensure I'm successful? Sometimes it might just be with yourself.

- Have I identified all stakeholders that will be involved within my strategy plan? Do I know who will support me and who might block me?
- Do I need to create a small brainstorming session or workshop to help me think this through?
- In essence, do I have a way forward to begin executing my own personal change strategy?

The second sense check comes directly from you. This one is very personal, and you are asking yourself if you have *Hope* or whether you know *How* you are going to execute your personal change strategy. During this time of critical reflection, you want to ask yourself the following:

Hope/How

- Do I have the right plan in place?
- Do I have others' buy in and support or are they still stuck in the SCARED model?
- Do I have the leadership support or approvals necessary for my strategy and options?

Note: If I answer no to any of the above, then I may want to revisit my strategy and options and rework some of them until I can say yes to all of these items. This is where the model is not linear. You may need to go back and forth just a bit before you complete your change strategy.

- If I'm ok with the above, then I can move forward.

If you find you are able to progress forward, then you can move on to the most important aspect of your SO WHAT plan. This part is asking yourself what *Actions* you will take to ensure you are successful. Some might think that actions are a sense check, but in reality, these are the milestones that you will take to ensure that your plan goes the way you want it to because of your change situation. For example, imagine you have just used Strategy, Options, and Way forward in planning a wedding. Do you stop there? No, you move forward and plan out the actions you need to take to ensure everything goes as you have planned. Likewise, what if you have decided you do not like the changes within your sales team that your supervisor has implemented? Let's say you have decided to quit. Hopefully you do not just quit without any plan. What is your plan? What's your strategy and what are your options? Do you have a way forward? Do you have hope or know how it will work? If yes, then great. What actions are you going to take?

Actions

- What actions do you need to take to ensure your strategy goes off smoothly?
- Who do you need to help from to take this plan forward? Do you need approvals, support, and are you ready to act?
- Begin your plan of action to include:
  - Leadership support for launching, communication process, implementation process. This may just be with yourself but can also include others.
  - What measures for success will you include?
  - Do you have a timeline and milestones?

The last portion of your SO WHAT plan may be the most important element outside of a good and solid strategy plan. This part is *taking ownership*. I have yet to see any of these elements let alone how the individual takes ownership of a change process reflected in any model. That is why I felt it so necessary to conclude the model with taking ownership being the breakout point to end the SO WHAT plan. The goal of SO WHAT is to ensure that you think your strategy through, vet it either with yourself or the support of others, and make an informed action on the decision that you have made. You are now taking control over personal change—your own personal change. In this final stage you want to reflect on the following:

Take ownership

- How will I hold myself accountable to execute my personal change plan?
- Who will I share my plan with and communicate so that I can be successful?
- Who will be my key stakeholders to check in with for support if needed?
- How will I know that progress is made and how will I report or share that?
- Will I check with others involved in my plan to ensure they have what they need? (Could be just with yourself—stop and reflect.)
- How will I see my plan through, and will I ask anyone for help if needed? Who would I ask?
- How will I celebrate any successes or regroup if necessary to support towards success?

These elements ensure that you are creating the process of critical reflection for yourself in navigating your own way through personal change. This is the SCARED SO WHAT methodology within two separate models that go together to ensure you have the ability to creatively process that critical reflection portion. The main action item that I am suggesting and is evidenced throughout my research is that we have the power to manage personal change. Instead of creating unnecessary worry, angst, stress, and anxiety over changeful situations, stop and think these situations through. By using the SCARED SO WHAT models, you are doing that. Think of it like solving a mathematical problem. We have many tools to facilitate that through division, multiplication, subtraction, addition, and other ways of solving situational issues. We can do the same for personal change by thinking through the elements of the change process.

SCARED is the first step in achieving this goal. We need to stop and look at and assess how we are feeling towards a change situation as it occurs if possible. That is not always the case and sometimes change is thrust upon us. Sometimes at work, our supervisors bring out one of these organizational change models and begin to tell us how we are going to make a change transition at work. Rarely do our sales leaders stop and ask us:

- Do you agree with this change that we are making?
- How do you feel about this change process?
- Do you think you can support this change?
- Are you onboard with this change?

More often than not, the supervisors just approach you either through a one-to-one session or in a team meeting and say, "Listen up, here's what's coming down the line." Ever heard that before? And for my sales leaders who are reading this book, do you ask your team these questions? If you do, then great for you! Sounds like you are one who really cares and has empathy for your sales members. But if you answer no, which is more often what I have found in my research, I ask you this question: "What happens if your sales member is not onboard with the changes you are making, and they don't tell you?" I'll tell you what happens. You have a recipe for a problem. And that problem could cost you dearly.

Whenever you want to launch a sales change or any change process you should ask yourself, "Do I care about what the team members think and feel?" You should. Because they are the ones that will be responsible for executing your change strategy. And if they are not onboard, then what will you do to get them onboard? And that's even if you know how they are feeling. The good news is that there are also tools to help you with using the SCARED SO WHAT process. SCARED comes with a questionnaire, so just by simply answering some questions you can get a printout and a visual aid on how some-one is feeling towards a change process that you may be imposing on them. Likewise, SO WHAT is the model that helps people to build out their own personal action plan for executing change. This model also has a template where someone can build out their own strategic plan. We will cover these tools in the next few chapters.

No matter if you choose to be a transformational leader and support your team members by using SCARED SO WHAT with them, or by giving it to them and helping them to learn how to manage personal change on their own, SCARED SO WHAT should be at the forefront of your mind in leading your sales teams through change at work, because change ultimately becomes personal no matter how you try not to make it. We are dealing with human beings, and the changes we impose upon them, with them, or for them affect them personally.

How have I used SCARED SO WHAT with my sales teams?

Within my organization I have freely given the SCARED SO WHAT model to all of my team members as well as the global heads of sales. Within this, I have also created a digital course that is about 30 minutes in length for them to take within our organization's learning management system. I teach this model to all of our sales members as a way of helping them gain control over the constant barrage of change they experience on a monthly, weekly, and daily basis. Within our organization we have constant sales strategy changes, promotional offerings, strategic drivers, operational changes, guest cancellations, and travel customers who may support us one week but not the next. There are business development deals and new contracts to try and secure, and within all of these items and actions come consistent sales rejections from potential clients and customers. This is hard on anyone, but for salespeople it is constant. I can no longer say to them, "Oh don't take it personally," because you and I both know that they will and do. Instead, the best gift and guidance I can give them through working transformationally is to further support their development by teaching them how to use critical reflection within the models so that they can process personal change for themselves.

I am not alone in this journey. Since launching this in 2019 and throughout the global pandemic, SCARED SO WHAT has also been used for our B2B customers. Our key account managers and retail managers as well as our sales enablement and support members have shared the model's features in hopes of helping our B2B partners and customers navigate their own bouts of personal change. We have had customers stating that they are not only using it at work but within their own families and with their children. I've had instances where customers have said their children are embracing this quickly because of their lack of experience and time with resistance to change. They are able to adjust to it faster and use critical reflection as a way of thinking things through. While I designed it for my sales team members across the globe, I have quickly found that this applies to just about everyone. Young, old, experienced, inexperienced, across cultures and languages, navigating personal change is something we can all benefit from. And in the next few chapters, I will break down just how you can use SCARED SO WHAT and go over the SCARED quiz and the SO WHAT template for you to learn and use as well.

Endnote

1 Unpublished interview with Ken Ross, President, Dr. Elisabeth Kübler-Ross Foundation, September 9, 2020.

06

Discovering emotions and actions using SCARED

Is all change scary? That answer really depends on the person the change involves. For some people, all change can be scary. And for others, it is more an independent situational difference. Dr. Carla Marie Manly (2021) says, "When we choose to create a change, such as moving to a new home or shifting jobs, we feel more in control of the outcome. If the change is brought about by forces outside of our control, whether a boss, a pandemic, or an accident, we feel disempowered." Daryl Conner (2012) says, "Change is easy when people like it." We have seen this in his models earlier, but he also has distinguished that people do not like change when they are not in control, or the change is imposed or unexpected. There is ample science and psychology to iterate that people are hardwired to fear or resist change, as Dr. Manly noted above. For extreme cases, as I have shared earlier, this is known as *metathesiophobia*, or the literal fear of change, and it can be crippling to those who have this. That being said, the model SCARED SO WHAT was designed to be used by anyone who is experiencing a change situation regardless of if it is within or outside of their control. It does not matter if the change is a happy one or one that is completely unexpected or negative. In my research in building the model, I make it very clear that one does not have to be scared to use the model. It is intended to be used to critically reflect on a change situation no matter if the change is a happy one, like choosing to get married or buying a new car, or an unexpected change, like being let go from a job. This reflection can be lengthy and well thought out or it can be achieved in quick time by thinking through the steps in the model. Either way, SCARED SO WHAT gives us the ability to learn how to effectively manage personal change for ourselves.

How do I use the SCARED portion of the model?

I truly believe that in each of us, to a certain extent, we possess the ability to manifest and master our own life's journey. However, I am not naive to the fact that many instances and events throughout our lives happen outside of our control. This is the result of constant change. If there is anything I would want you to understand at this point, it is that we do have the ability to affect the outcomes of changes that happen to us. This is achieved through critical reflection (McNiff, 2013), sometimes in the moment (in action) or after the moment (on action). I propose that those outcomes can be measured through energy levels of either positive energy, neutral energy, or negative energy. On the one hand we can accept and embrace change; on the other, we can outright reject changes that happen to us. Sometimes we are indifferent to the changes we experience. However, because of our ability to choose, different outcomes can occur due to the changes we experience. SCARED is the critical reflection tool that can help you to break down what you are feeling (in action) or what you felt (on action) during or as a result of a change situation. The end goal is for you to have performed some Actions and Explored some options or have used critical reflection as a way to make a decision about what you are feeling. This results in making an "informed" decision. That means you did not just merely react to the change and make an assumption or uncover a reaction, you took the time to think it through, assess your options or possible outcomes, ask questions, and seek information to support your thought process and come to a decision based on the information attained. Please allow me to explain first how the SCARED model is designed to be used, then I will share a few examples of how I have used the SCARED portion of the model within my sales force.

As illustrated in Chapter 5, the model is not linear in any way. The points that are fixed are at the center. This is where you are at the center of the model and the change you either are experiencing or have experienced is tied directly to you. For this matter, the change as the action agent is at the center of the model. You and the change situation are tied together because the feelings that the change emotes are yours.

You can see this in Figure 6.1 (which we have repeated from Chapter 5). The center of the model is your starting point. It is here that you can use the model during a change situation that is happening to you or even after a change situation has just occurred or has happened in the past. You first need to put yourself at the center of your own inquiry and then identify to yourself what exactly is the change. This is the art of critical reflection either in action or on actions that have happened already. And this leads you to your own understanding of how to manage personal change. Start with you!

In the outer band of the model are various reflection opportunities. You can see that there is a curved line just after decision or indecision point. This line is the end goal of using the model and I will talk more about that a little further on. The suggested starting

FIGURE 6.1 The SCARED Wheel of Change

point is at the top center, titled Surprise. From there, one would normally go clockwise or to the right in a process of reflection upon the change. Think of it like being your own coach. You use each point in the model to ask yourself open-ended questions that may begin with "What am I...?" "How am I...?" "Do I feel...?" and then reflect on your own answers. As we are all individuals, we have the right to think for ourselves. That theme is the very purpose of this model—to incorporate the individual's own ability to choose versus a model that is prescriptive of an outcome. With that in mind, one can bounce back and forth or skip a point entirely. However, the main purpose of this model is to allow the user to stop and critically reflect on a change situation, so that they learn how to embrace change and ultimately manage it to make informed decisions that enhance their own journey and outcomes.

S—Surprise

If we begin here, when reflecting on a change that either is happening, perhaps is going to happen if known, or something that has happened in the past, one might ask, "Am I surprised by this change?" or "What level of surprise does this change represent to me?"

As a starting point, one would reflect on their own individual feelings towards the change being a surprise whether it be positive, neutral, or negative. This is a starting point for giving an indication of how you might be feeling overall towards the change. If you are positively surprised, then you might be leaning towards a favorable outcome. If your reaction is not really positive or negative or the change that is happening was known to you, then you may be indifferent to it and this could be represented by the neutral state. If the change is known, some people may bypass this stage of reflection, but I would encourage people to embrace full critical reflection and that involves how someone learns about the change as well.

C—Champion or Conflicted

Once we understand our initial reaction to the change, we then start to formulate our initial feelings towards what is occurring.

This is where we begin to become reactive and work through our emotions. Our emotions (McLeod, 2020) are reflected as defense mechanisms, as Dr. Sigmund Freud uncovered in the late 1800s. His work was carried on through his daughter Anna Freud in the 1930s and onward. Since then, many psychologists and researchers have tied many defense mechanisms back to our emotions as a way of helping us process and cope with change. On the positive side of change, one could identify with the word Champion. It is here that people can ask themselves, "Do I favor or champion this change, or do I like it?" Likewise, if the change is something that is not altogether too exciting or does not illicit a positive or negative emotion, then one could be indifferent to the change, and this can be a neutral energy reaction. "It doesn't bother me either way," might be something someone says at this point.

The opposite side is the negative energy spectrum. At this point one might be feeling poorly about the change situation and if they do not have all the information necessary to reflect or formulate a decision, they may be Conflicted. This word conflicted, although not necessarily negative or bad, simply means confusion or lack of clarity or certainty. It does not mean that one will remain there. It simply means they are lacking either information or the ability to think positively about the situation at that moment. More information is needed to affect a different outcome. At this point, it is important to know that there is no right or wrong. Everyone's journey in receiving or participating in a change event is personal and unique. They will ultimately decide how they act or react towards the change situation they are experiencing. At this moment, they are assessing where they may be in a critical reflection process. It is encouraged to sense out and feel all emotions to uncover the full scenario of the change.

A—Actions

Within the sales career pathway, we can easily identify with the term Actions and often associate it simultaneously with activities. What actions or activities can we do each day to create revenue generation scenarios or to increase our pipeline, is how we in sales often reflect.

Action drives performance. This is very commonplace throughout the sales arena. The same goes for personal change and at this point in the SCARED model, actions are at the very heart of helping the individual to make an informed decision versus simply guessing or assuming. This is a stopping point for the individual in their own instance of critical reflection to perform an action that generates information. An action in sales is to generate an opportunity, albeit to increase relationships, build pipeline, facilitate a revenue generating opportunity, or to close a sale. The same process towards personal change is to generate an action that illustrates or gleans information. We can achieve this by asking questions either of ourselves or to others about the change we are experiencing. This could be in the form of an email, phone call, virtual meeting, performing an online search, researching printed articles or books—any action to seek clarity for understanding. Any type of action to bring in new information is warranted at this point. As we discussed in earlier chapters, in the emocracy, people are making buying decisions based on emotions, such as how they feel, or how they identify towards a product, a company, or a service that is offered. They do not typically research fact and information to help them assess what is best for their needs, rather they react and buy based on emotions. We need to do the opposite when it comes to understanding how personal change affects us. And that is to generate actions so that we can bring in new information to help us understand how the change affects us in order to allow us to make an informed decision. Simply put, actions generate information.

R—Receptive or Rejective

Hopefully, a person using the model will reflect on all stages and take the time to absorb and learn from the change situation thoroughly. But as I mentioned earlier, people can skip through the model and bounce back and forth, such is the way we learn. This next stage is where we reflect if we are receptive of the change situation at hand, representing positive energy, or if we reject it, representing negative energy. Again, try not to get too concerned with the positive or negative aspect of it at this moment. Regardless of which way one might be leaning, this represents the individual's right to choose their own outcome. Not every change is for everyone. But everyone will have their own SO WHAT to uncover as a result of their choices.

On the positive side, Receptive simply means that you are agreeable with the change that is happening, will happen, or has happened to you. From here, you are confident, encouraged, and on your way towards being accepting of this change. At this stage, one might not have come to a full decision as of yet, but they are leaning towards being favorable of the change occurrence. People can also just "go with the flow". This means that they are indifferent to the change. As an example, have you ever implemented a change with your sales team and a particular member does not show happiness or anger but merely says, "Sure, tell me what to do," and acts indifferent? Perhaps the change being imposed is on the neutral state to them and they simply prefer to just enact the changes you prescribe.

The negative reaction to the change situation is a form of rejection. It is here in this stage that a person is saying that they do not agree with the change or that the change being imposed is not for them. I must stress that this is not about being right or wrong. People have the ability and the right to reject change. Not every change that occurs is magically going to be accepted. And this is the point I argued aggressively in my master's program. For those that do reject change, how do we support them? Do we even know if they reject the changes I as a sales leader impose upon them? What about changes from customers to the salespeople? What if my sales team reject changes our B2B customers make? This point is very important. It is easy for the individual to identify with positive change but what about negative changes? What happens if they reject? For the individual, this is a critical point because depending on what actions they took, they could be misinformed, or they could be adequately informed. There are a lot of "ifs" at this stage. But for the individual, if they jump ahead to make a negative decision, they might rob themselves of a positive opportunity. Likewise, if a supervisor is not aware of a person that has rejected an imposed change, they may lose out on the team member's motivation, participation, support, and could ultimately lose out on revenue generation or suffer the loss of an employee by them leaving the organization. Rejection of change from an individual's point of view is a critical step in assessing understanding of change. What I would encourage you to do at this point is as follows:

- If you are receptive of the change, great! Move on to the next phase and possibly right on to making a favorable decision.

- If you are rejective of the change, stop and give yourself another action opportunity by exploring other options to ensure you can make an informed decision for yourself. You might say, "This change isn't for me," and that is fine. But give yourself every opportunity to be certain. You owe it to yourself to make the best decision for *you*.

E—Explore options

In sales management, we do not simply stop when we have discovered, implemented, or reviewed sales actions one time. We continuously perform more and more sales actions and activities. We conduct brainstorming sessions internally within our sales teams to foster new ideas. We interact with our marketing counterparts to learn how they can illustrate our ideas and make them come to fruition. We facilitate fact-finding sessions with our customers to garnish their wants and needs, gain feedback of products and services, and find out ways they wish to be sold to. All of this is done in efforts to continuously perform actions to generate information that will help us lead to a successful outcome. Managing personal change is no different. Just because we have performed a few actions, does not mean that we cannot come up with a different outcome or change our minds. Quite the contrary. If we are leaning towards a negative approach and are rejecting the change situation at hand, performing additional actions through exploring further options or opportunities can generate different outcomes or further support our feelings and guidance we have already reflected upon. This is a point for you to further your understanding of a change situation. This can be achieved by asking yourself:

- Are there any other options or opportunities for me to consider this change?

- Is there anyone else I could go to for advice or guidance?

- If I am rejective of this change, what could be the potential outcomes?
- Am I prepared to accept the outcomes? If yes, the move forward. If no, then what other options or opportunities might you be able to uncover?

Note that this is not a prescribed approach to try and make you make a positive decision. This is your own journey, and should you not accept the change situation you are experiencing or have experienced—that is ok! Change is personal. It is all about you. The goal is for you to make the best possible decision you can but to be able to say that you have given it full reflection, consideration, and thought. No matter what you decide, you will still have your own SO WHAT to create to implement or achieve your own change. Neither I, nor any other human being, can prescribe or tell you how you are going to think. You must do that for yourself. And that is why this model is a reflective, non-linear model that incorporates your ability to accept or reject change.

D—Decision/Indecision

Ideally, we are getting towards the end point of understanding your own feelings and navigating your way through personal change. Notice I said "ideally." This would be the goal. But again, I cannot prescribe how any one person is going to act or react towards a change situation. While the ideal outcome is that they make a favorable decision, they will make the decision based on what is right for them. That could be favorable and accepting of the change or unfavorable and rejective of the change.

From a supervisor's perspective: a leader might want to know if their team members are acceptive or rejective of the changes occurring because of either leadership directives or through B2B customer interactions. Knowing who the change adaptors are is beneficial because one can embrace them and champion them to help enact the changes. Likewise, the opposite is true. Knowing who is not acceptive of the change is an opportunity to either help someone gain more information and possibly generate a different outcome, or to help them in how they might participate or be a better support to the business goals and operation. Knowing who does not accept your changes could help to further develop someone or help them navigate their own way forward. Hopefully that can be within the company or organization. But if not, then be a transformational leader and help them to grow where they want to be even if that means outside the organization. The goal is to grow, develop, and retain valuable talent within the organization.

From the individual's perspective: knowing if you are favorable or unfavorable of the change and have formulated your decision based on critical reflection will ultimately help you to move onward in developing your own SO WHAT plan of action. If you champion the change, then you will naturally move forward to create your plan in support of that change. Likewise, if you reject the change, you will still ask yourself, "So what does this mean for me?" or "So what can I do about it?" Creating your own SO WHAT plan gives you the greatest opportunity for a successful outcome, whatever you deem success to be.

There is, however, another outcome that can happen. Have you ever heard someone say or said to yourself, "I'm not sure how I feel about this" or "I don't know what to do"? This can happen when individuals are stuck in what is called *indecision*. Simply put, it means that people cannot decide. They are confused about the information taken in. More often, in my research, the people with this outcome have not spent an adequate amount of time, if any time at all, focusing on actions or exploring options or opportunities. They have perhaps become stuck in the process, or maybe have not advanced through it at all, or have bypassed these two important features designed to evoke information that will aid them in facilitating the decision-making process. Indecision can lead a person back into the model at various stages. Often times, when I encounter someone that is in this situation, I turn to coaching and ask them, "What actions do you think you can do to find information?" or "Have you explored any options or opportunities to gain information?" and begin the conversation from there. But by the same token, if an individual finds themselves in this situation, they are encouraged to reflect on these two action items for themselves. Gaining further information will support them in making a decision regardless of the outcome. Being a leader, and supporting them to find their own actions through a coaching practice, can further their own development and possibly towards a favorable decision. Regardless the outcome, as a supervisor, you want to know where they stand.

How has the SCARED model been used in sales?

Since its inception in early 2019, the SCARED SO WHAT model has been used primarily in a global sales setting within the hospitality industry and primarily during the global pandemic known as Covid-19 and beyond. While it has been shared and utilized outside of the hospitality industry within other global sales business settings it has also been published and shared within the sales university educational aspect. My primary responsibility is within sales and supporting global sales teams within cruise, hospitality, and travel industry related areas. We have utilized SCARED SO WHAT in championing our sales members' own ability to manage and navigate their own way through personal change primarily in their sales roles. As a result, SCARED SO WHAT has also been shared within our B2B travel agency sales customers for their own use during this same timeframe and continues to be shared as of this writing. From travel agents to territory managers, key account managers, business development managers, sales leaders, and sales support roles, learning how to manage change is fostering critical reflection and the ability to develop people in thinking change through for themselves in a more informed fashion. But it doesn't just stop within the sales arena, nor the hospitality industry.

Below are real-life examples of how SCARED SO WHAT has been used within our sales environment. These examples are real and are related to sales, but I challenge you to think of examples for yourselves, and discuss with others on your team or perhaps even in your family and personal lives how you might be able to use the models for yourselves and your team members.

EXAMPLE 1: A POSITIVE CHANGE SCENARIO THAT COULD HAVE
BEEN PERCEIVED AS NEGATIVE: SUBJECT WAS ON INCENTIVE
CHANGE

In late 2019, the cruise industry came to a complete halt due to the
pandemic (Martinez, 2021). For a period of almost 18 months (Holland et
al., 2021) there were no cruise ships sailing with any paying passengers
and, as a result, revenue opportunities were significantly diminished. The
cruise industry has multiple booking windows and opportunities. There are
late bookers who make their travel decisions very late and want to go
within a few months. There are also further out bookers who like to plan
their vacation experiences between 12 to 18 months in advance. We know
this to be true from monitoring the booking curve and actions of our
consumers. The decision to book a vacation experience is very personal and
individual—much like change. But for us during the lockdown, when ships
were not able to sail, our sales window shifted more towards a further out
approach looking towards the next few years. As a result, our sales team
members and travel agency customers still had products and services to
sell. But this meant that our sales incentives needed to change to shift
focus and drive the right business behavior needed to support our end
customers, our travel agency customers, and our business needs to stay
afloat.

This also meant that the drivers to support the behaviors necessary to
facilitate everyone's goals needed to be shifted—that is, the sales
incentives needed to shift as well to be favorable to all involved. We had to
think about our sales employees' wellbeing, their ability to earn a living
and support themselves and their families, as well as to serve the needs of
the business. We had to be inclusive of the sales employees' needs and
ensure stability so they could earn a living while we were not currently
sailing with paying customers. This meant a massive shift, or change, in the
sales incentive program needed to occur.

Even though the new sales incentive would generate the ability for our
sales team members to earn more money now versus the existing plan,
there were mumblings throughout that a possible incentive change created
some discord for a few of the sales members. Change for the sake of
change can make people uncomfortable. For a certain number of people,
change will always be perceived as negative and that, no matter what the
change is, it cannot be good for them. Knowing this, we decided to

re-emphasize the SCARED SO WHAT methodology of absorbing personal change. I created a digital learning model in our company's learning management system (LMS) that was just under 30 minutes in length and rolled this out prior to communicating the new incentive change. We ensured everyone had proper time to participate, absorb, and facilitate discussions on how to use SCARED SO WHAT and reflect on personal change. Shortly thereafter, we communicated the new sales incentive program with the team members and used the model as a way of discussing it through with them. In a coaching fashion, using open-ended questions, myself and other supervisors could ask, "How do you feel about the change?" "Are you surprised by the change?" "What actions could you take to learn more about the change?" "Are you receptive or rejective of the change?" as well as questions regarding their decision-making due to the change.

Throughout, some people were concerned about their ability to maintain their incentives and how the change would impact them. Even though the change itself was designed to put more money into their hands now so they could support themselves during this downturn, some people did react negatively simply because it was a change. Through the process of helping them think it through, critically reflecting and assessing for themselves, the team was able to help not only themselves, but to help others with their own understanding of how the change would impact them in a short-term, positive way to support their earning potential. Overall, we experienced early adoption and next to no negativity versus other situations of incentive changes rolled out at other times that were thought of as favorable as well. The key to success in implementing even a positive message was the inclusion of the individuals on their own journey of understanding how this change would affect them. By merely taking into account our sales team members' own individualities, we achieved rapid adoption and acceptance, and provided support to help those who at first resisted the changes. This is an example of inclusive leadership and bringing the individuals along on the journey. At the same time, we also used one of the organizational change models described in earlier chapters as a change management process model. But we took the time to include SCARED SO WHAT as a way to bring the individuals into the change management process as well.

EXAMPLE 2: NEW RULES FOR OUR TRAVEL AGENCY CUSTOMERS AROUND HOW TO RE-BOOK A CRUISE THAT WAS CANCELLED BECAUSE OF THE PANDEMIC

The global pandemic brought about constant change not only for our sales team members, but also our travel agency customers and the sailing guests (customers) themselves. Countless thousands and thousands of guests had cruises booked throughout our fleets around the world. And all of a sudden, those voyages became cancelled. This meant that due to the pandemic and the cancellation of voyages, new rules and regulations on how to support customers were necessary. While the sales team members themselves were already learning how to use the SCARED SO WHAT methodology and framework, our travel agency customers would soon be able to benefit from the discussion and reflection models as well.

The normal terms and conditions that apply to the use of airline tickets, hotels, transportation, car rentals, tours, and cruise voyages could no longer apply. The situation at hand was a global change impact that was not the fault of either the supplier nor the end customer and, as such, new rules and ways of working to support customers had to occur. Many airlines and hotels were trying to react to their customers' demands and simple cancellation policies were no longer effective. The same applied towards cruise reservations and bookings, which had to change as well. But we decided not only to roll out new rules of what a travel agency customer could do with existing bookings, but also a way to help them navigate all of this personal change affecting them as well within their own businesses and livelihoods in working together with us in the travel sector.

Through a program known as RCL CARES, my team at Royal Caribbean Group designed a whole new approach to support our B2B customer—our travel agents. In this approach, we put together programs of support for our travel agency customers so they could easily find, source, and absorb the new rules as they applied to them and their customers. We also put SCARED SO WHAT out for them to participate and join in on the journey in managing personal change in support of themselves. This was done through a digital campaign in where travel agents could learn about "Selling beyond Covid-19" (Van Ulbrich, 2020a), whereby SCARED SO WHAT was built as an online course they could freely participate in, and our sales team members could engage with them in managing their own change situations. The work involved by all team members was pioneered through our UK sales division leadership, but ultimately allowed our travel customers not only an accessible way to find out how and what to do with existing cancelled reservations, but also how they could be supported from a financial and physical aspect in an emotional and change management process that would be self-transforming for them and their business communities. From April to September 2020 a total of 1,148 travel agency customers actively engaged in the SCARED SO WHAT course. This resulted in both our sales team members and travel agency customers co-facilitating their own conversations about change together. The result was that we had brought our travel agency customers along the same journey that was happening within our own sales team members in navigating change. Thus, they were able to get on board and foster the changes in a greater capacity and lead themselves to the best possible outcome for everyone involved. It was here that many travel agents even shared how they were not only using the models for themselves, but also for their families and children who were also making their own ways through the results of the pandemic.

There are countless more opportunities to share how SCARED SO WHAT is and has been used within our sales teams. From deal negotiation to deal rejection, changes in global organizational structure, to the redesign of job roles and clarity of functions. The cruise industry was victim to countless job layoffs and workforce reductions, as was almost every industry. But one might argue that the hospitality industry was hit the hardest as almost all travel came to a near halt—the cruise industry came to a complete halt for just over 18 months. Change within, for, and around our sales team members was constant—even to the way we had to sell in the new virtual sales environment, selling from home in our pajama and sweatpant bottoms with a nice shirt and sometimes a suit jacket or blouse on top. Sales did not stop. It transformed. And SCARED SO WHAT helped us to embrace that change transformation and move forward.

Now we know how to use it—is there a simpler way?

There is almost always an easier way to do things. And using the SCARED model for identifying and understanding how we might be feeling towards a change situation can be an easy process as well. I have created a SCARED quiz (Van Ulbrich, 2020b) to help us all reflect on a change situation within the moment. The quiz is free for all to use and consists of easy questions that give a ranking score from zero to seven. Before we begin the quiz, we need to reflect on what the change is and how we are feeling about it. If you know the root cause or exactly what is causing the change, that is best for you to put at the center of your mind and reflect upon when answering the quiz questions. Once you have the change scenario in mind, then you can begin to scan the questions and provide a rating for each item.

The questions are designed to capture your feelings on each aspect within the SCARED model. This is based on your actions and your behavior and produces a result at the very end so you can easily gain a perspective on what you are feeling. This process can reveal areas of opportunity and can also confirm an outcome of your reflective thinking on a particular change topic.

Remember, this applies to all types of change situations regardless of if it is positive or negative. With your change scenario in mind, you can then answer and rank the questions accordingly. Zero means the question does not apply to you at all. Seven means the question applies to you perfectly. And somewhere in the middle between zero and seven is how you would rate the question as it applies to you.

Once you have answered all the questions, the graph will jump back to the top of the screen indicating that you have completed the questionnaire. You will want to then scroll down to the bottom where you can see your results. The questions should take you no more than 7 to 10 minutes if you reflect and answer each question honestly. This will not work to your best advantage if you simply fly through the questions. You need to give a little thought to each question for it to have the most realistic outcome for you. Many of us are visual learners and a change situation is a learning opportunity as well. Seeing how you score yourself through the SCARED quiz can help you to further asses your change situation more easily. So, what do the possible results mean? Let us look at an example of a SCARED quiz result to gain a better understanding of how it works (see Figure 6.2).

FIGURE 6.2 The SCARED quiz

My SCARED Quiz Results: WHERE AM I IN THIS CHANGE PROCESS?

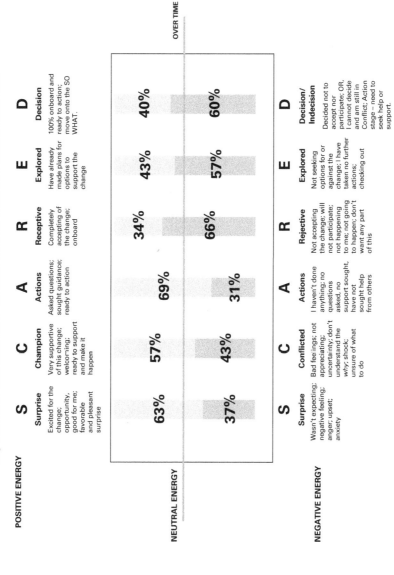

POSITIVE ENERGY

S	C	A	R	E	D
Surprise	**Champion**	**Actions**	**Receptive**	**Explored**	**Decision**
Excited for the change; opportunity, good for me; favorable and pleasant surprise	Very supportive of this change; welcoming; ready to support and make it happen	Asked questions; sought guidance; ready to action	Completely accepting of the change; onboard	Have already made plans for options to support the change	100% onboard and ready to action; move onto the SO WHAT.

S	C	A	R	E	D
63%	57%	69%	34%	43%	40%

NEUTRAL ENERGY

S	C	A	R	E	D
37%	43%	31%	66%	57%	60%

NEGATIVE ENERGY

S	C	A	R	E	D
Surprise	**Conflicted**	**Actions**	**Rejective**	**Explored**	**Decision/ Indecision**
Wasn't expecting; negative feeling; anger; upset; anxiety	Bad feelings; not appreciating; uncertainty; don't understand the why; shock; unsure of what to do	I haven't done anything; no questions asked, no support sought, have not sought help from others	Not accepting the change; will not participate; not happening to me; not going to happen; don't want any part of this	Not seeking options for or against the change; I have taken no further actions; checking out	Decided not to accept nor participate; OR, I cannot decide and am still in Conflict; Action stage – need to seek help or support.

OVER TIME

On the left side of the quiz results, you will notice that the results are broken down by their reflective energy state. On the top left you will see Positive Energy; in the middle left, you will see Neutral Energy; and on the bottom left you will see Negative Energy. From there, if we focus on the positive energy side, you will see across the top grid the reflective questions of SCARED and their corresponding definitions. In the middle of the results, you will notice a bar, with levels of either light or dark gray. Light gray (the top portion of each bar) indicates a favorable viewpoint or that much consideration has been given to this element. Dark gray (the bottom portion of each bar) indicates a less-favorable viewpoint or that less actions, options, or consideration has been given to this element.

The bottom of the graph represents the Negative Energy results. Across the bottom of the grid, you will notice corresponding letters that represent the negative energy spectrum. Remember, this is not literally negative. It is just an indication that one might be either leaning towards a negative reaction or they have not given any or enough consideration or participation towards that specific element. For example, if within Surprise you see mostly light gray (over 55 percent at minimum), then you could safely reflect that you are feeling positive about this change situation. Likewise, if you see more light gray indications in Champion, you can reflect the same. If you see a higher percentage of light gray in Actions, this indicates that you have achieved measurable actions towards finding more information about the change situation you are experiencing. The same can be attributed to the other elements. Light gray equals positive energy and the more light gray it is, the more likely you are to be favorable towards the change situation.

If, by chance, you find your results are bordering the 50/50 percentage mark, this can indicate indecision. An easy way to change this outcome for yourself is to focus on additional actions and explore the further opportunities you can take to understand and assess the change situation you are reviewing. If you retake the quiz, you most likely will come to a different outcome because you have obtained a new understanding of the change itself.

But what if you have a lot of dark gray? Remember, there is no right or wrong answer here. The purpose of the SCARED quiz is for you to easily identify how you are feeling during a change situation or as a result of using critical reflection. These are just indicators and show you a visual example of your feelings. You still have the power to change them by performing more actions or exploring more opportunities if you want to. You have two options:

OPTION A

If you see a greater percentage of dark gray in every line item of SCARED, then you most likely have not given enough consideration to Actions nor Explored any options or opportunities. I would encourage you not to simply go with this outcome. Rather, you want to see Actions and Explore with as a high a percentage of light gray as possible. This indicates that you have thought the situation through and have given yourself ample support of finding out information to make an informed decision. Try to facilitate some or more actions by asking for support or advice to gain information. Likewise, be sure to explore all options and opportunities before you simply rush to a decision. Then, retake the quiz and see if you have a different outcome. You should notice a change as a result of your efforts. From there, you can begin to formulate a decision.

OPTION B

If you see a greater percentage of dark gray in Surprise, Conflicted, Rejective, and Decision, but your Actions and Explore are have a higher percentage of light gray, this means that you have given considerable thought, taken actions to become more informed, but you have decided to reject the change. That is ok. You still will need to build your own plan of action of what you will do about this change.

The quiz is a simple way to view your actions or inactions as a result of critically reflecting on a change situation you are experiencing or one that may come in the future or one in the past. This is the first step in using the SCARED process as a way of learning how to manage and navigate personal change. You have many options to choose from in learning how to reflect critically for yourself. I personally have simply written down each letter on a napkin on an airplane flight to reflect on a change situation happening to me. From there, I started to etch out my SO WHAT plan as well. No matter how you use it, whether in thinking it out to yourself, writing it down, or taking the quiz, as you learn how to use the SCARED model in understanding your own experiences with personal change, you are learning how to take control of yourself and your personal change situation. That is a very important thing that we have not learnt from our parents or in generations gone by. The next part is probably the most important element. Once you understand how you are feeling towards a personal change situation, you need to decide what you can or will do about it rather than worrying or panicking. Creating your own SO WHAT plan for actioning change can be a freeing event for you. But before that happens, there is usually a gap between making a decision about a change and what comes next. Coming up in Chapter 7, we will explore that gap between decision-making and the SO WHAT model for actioning change.

07

The gap between decision and action

Have you ever found yourself at work, stuck in a sales meeting where a change to remove a longstanding promotional offer for your accounts has just been shared? If, as I suspect, this has happened to you, what do you do next? You will likely go back to your desk to make an action plan for communicating this change with your accounts. All the while, you are sitting there staring at the computer with your fingers at the keyboard ready to share the bad news, but you just cannot hit any keys to start the message. Have you ever found yourself at the vending machine, at the coffee shop, or at the speaker box at the fast-food drive through... or even standing in front of your own refrigerator, thinking to yourself, "What do I want?" Have you ever stopped to consider how many times you ask yourself this question?

Psychologists suggest we make over 35,000 decisions in a day (Krockow, 2018). William James (1890) said: "The mind is at every stage a theatre of simultaneous possibilities." That leads me to ask what it is that influences our decisions. What influences us to make a decision and choose an action or outcome over any other possibility? At every instance, our minds are continuously rationalizing and processing data input in order to stimulate an action from our bodies. That can be an action of speech, further thought, or even a physical movement. And that can be for things that we know we already like and are willing to do or want!

But what happens if the stimulus that is occurring to us is in the form of a change process? Think about that for a minute. What if it is a good change? Will you still question it? What if it is a negative or bad change? What do you do? Better yet, what do you want? This has been researched extensively over time, and the literature research is plentiful. What is the gap between decision and action? Research conducted by Wispinsky, Gallivan, and Chapman (2020) concluded that decision-making is a competition between choice and options. The outcome of that competition is that "decision making is a single and gradual process that begins with the presentation (or consideration) of choice options and continues throughout movement execution" (Wispinski, Gallivan, and Chapman, 2020). So, what does all of that mean? In the most simplistic terms before completing an action, we question ourselves over the possibilities and choices we have to consider and act on. We do this upwards of 35,000 times per day. And that is for everyday, conscious and unconscious consideration points. Ponder this, have you ever decided what you were going to grab out of your refrigerator and then, upon opening it, reached for something else? Of course. We do this all the time. But what we can do better is to learn how to manage change in support of making informed decisions.

As we have uncovered in earlier chapters, SCARED is the model for stopping and taking a critical reflection about a change situation. The person experiencing the change should stop and ask themselves questions to inspire critical reflection:

S: Surprise. Am I surprised about this change? Is it a positive or negative surprise? Or does it really matter to me? That is, am I neutral to it?

C: Champion/Conflict. Am I conflicted or do I champion this change? Conflict is a negative feeling, or a concern. Champion is a positive feeling of positivity about the change. Likewise, if I am uncertain, it could be neutral.

A: Actions. What actions can I take to gain more information about this change? Many actions are positive energy. Some actions are neutral. Little or no action is negative.

R: Receptive/Rejective. How am I feeling about this change? Am I receptive or do I reject it?

E: Explore. Can I explore any further options or opportunities as a result of this change? Is there any more information I could gain to help in making an informed decision?

D: Decision. Have I made a favorable decision? Am I not able to make a decision? Indecision? Have I made an unfavorable decision?

What is a favorable decision?

On the point of decision-making you have multiple scenarios. If the change at hand is favorable and a change that you are happy to support, then most likely you are feeling very comfortable about it. But even though it is favorable you still want to ensure that you perform actions necessary to gain all information about that change situation so you can tell yourself that you made an informed decision. You never want to assume that you know all of the answers and possible outcomes. Seek clarity to support and ensure you have the facts necessary to carry out and help you stand by your favorable decision.

What does indecision mean?

Sometimes we do not have all of the information and yet, maybe, we do. But we find ourselves stuck in a situation of saying to ourselves, "I don't know what to do." In this instance, perhaps, you have some more actions that can be taken. Even the simple task of asking open-ended questions on the change process to a sales leader or your other sales team members can help elicit data points for your consideration. Exploring additional options or opportunities as a result of that change by reading, asking, calling others, or listening to others speak on the topic can produce additional guidance. Indecision is the lack of information needed to choose a direction. Or perhaps it is the opposite and you have too much information that is countering the possible outcomes. Again, seeking guidance from others can help you make an informed decision.

What does it mean to make an unfavorable decision?

A decision to not accept the change imposed on or presented to you is not necessarily a bad decision. It simply means that this change is not for you, and you do not accept it. Depending on the change situation at hand, this could be the best decision for you and your needs. There is an old saying that says "Trust your instincts". Not all changes are for everyone, and should you find yourself in a situation of change that you do not agree with, then perhaps this change is not for you. You need to decide what you are or are not willing to accept. It does not mean that you have to quit your job or walk away. There are many decisions that a company can make that you might not agree with. You need to assess if you can tolerate, support, or perform the changes required. And you need to decide which ones you simply cannot tolerate. That may lead you to a different course of action. The key here is to make an informed decision based on facts and evidence to support your decision. Decisions based on assumptions can be disastrous for all involved, and most importantly, for you.

Understanding the framework behind SCARED can help empower you to ask yourself the right questions that inspire critical self-reflection. The key is not to make assumptions or to ignore what your body and mind are telling you about a change scenario, but rather to look at it face on and assess your feelings so that you can make the best decision possible for you and possibly others. Let's break this down into something simpler to understand. Everyone has lunch and sometimes brings their lunch with them to work. What happens if it goes missing?

Personal change: who stole my lunch?

Bringing lunch with us to work is something we all can easily identify with, so let us use this as an example of using the SCARED model. Pretend with me for a moment that you take your lunch with you to work each day. Never mind that at home, while preparing your lunch in the morning or the evening prior, you stood in front of your refrigerator and asked yourself, "What will I want tomorrow?" But having decided what you wanted, you then took the time to prepare it, and then took it to work and put it in the breakroom refrigerator. What if, at lunchtime, you walk to the breakroom and open the refrigerator only to find that your lunch is gone, and the refrigerator is empty? You thought your lunch would be there because you took the time to put it there. Hence, you reached for the door and decided to open it. But perhaps someone else from work reached in and took your lunch. Or even worse, the cleaning crew decided to toss out everything and clean it that day! What are you thinking then? This is a personal change situation, albeit a rather straightforward one. I mean... it's lunch! This can cause a major crisis in your mind. Now, let's break down this very simple, yet frustrating, case of personal change.

S: Surprise. Were you surprised? Yes? How did it make you feel? Angry. *My emotions are negative. I'm upset that someone would take my food.*

C: Champion/Conflict. Were you conflicted? *Yes, I am certainly not championing the fact someone took my lunch.*

A: Actions. What actions did you take? *None! I'm furious—someone took my lunch!*

R: Receptive/Rejective. Were you receptive of this? *Are you kidding? I'm rejecting the situation! Someone took my lunch, and I'm hungry.*

E: Explore. Did you explore any options? *What options? Someone took my lunch!*

D: Decision. Did you make a decision? *Yes, and I'm going to find out who did this. Someone is going to be in trouble.*

In this situation, just by observing the behavior and answers, we can safely say that a decision was made about having the lunch taken, and it was not a favorable one. The surprise level is negative and perhaps rightfully so.

When we take the time to do something, but the outcome is not what was expected, this can result in a negative response. Likewise, since you are not happy with this change situation you are perhaps conflicted as stated. What is interesting is that there are little to no actions taken—mostly an assumption that someone has taken the lunch, and the assumption is negative because of the lack of information. The only known fact is that the lunch is missing. In this case, you are rejecting the fact that your lunch is gone, and you are assuming that someone took it away from you. If I look at the explore options, none have been taken. And in this one instance, no options have been explored because you find yourself stuck in anger that your lunch is gone. Decision made? Yes, you guessed it. It's a negative decision and you are not happy at all. Did I summarize that correctly? If you agree with this situation or summary and you are saying, "Right on... I'd be mad too if someone took my lunch," then I ask you... have you made an informed decision? Stop and think for a moment. Have you made an *informed* decision? Or are you simply reacting to the situation or change that has occurred?

In this example, the answers provided to the SCARED questioning invoked a negative decision. The decision was based on assumptions without any actions or exploring possible options to seek out information. The decision was a negative one and made the person involved severely upset. Your lunch was stolen! What if you could take action to determine who took your lunch? Where would you start? A co-worker? The cleaning staff? The security team? Of course, someone could do all of these things. Any sort of questioning would help them make an informed decision about the situation.

But in this instance, it seems so obvious that someone took it for themselves, and they are justifiably upset or downright angry. How hard can this be? Someone has taken the lunch, right? Of course you would be upset.

But does the fact that the lunch is missing mean that it is really gone? Therein lies the question. Yes, someone could have taken it and eaten it for themselves. But if you stop to explore other options or opportunities to ask questions, what if you could find out who took it? What if the person taking it had a specific reason? What if a soda can spilled on everyone's lunch and ruined it? What if it was fine and the cleaning staff have moved it to another refrigerator? What if it was taken or ruined and someone was willing to take them to lunch or buy something for them as a replacement? There is an endless array of outcomes that could happen. But if you just stay angry and make decisions based on assumptions, you are not making an informed decision. Make sense? And that was just a change example about lunch!

So let us look at another change situation that is more relevant to sales and our daily work lives. Jayne is an account manager in a global sales function leading strategic accounts for the Sunshine Umbrella Solutions company. She has just returned to her desk from a sales meeting. In that meeting, the sales leadership decided to remove a longstanding promotional offer that had been very successful for Jayne and the sales team to use in creating sales deals for their accounts. Jayne's manager instructed her (and everyone else on her team) to immediately notify all accounts of the change via written communication using email. Back at her desk, Jayne begins to contemplate how she is going to notify her accounts about this situation, but she feels stuck. And here lies the gap between decision and action.

As a sales leader, during that sales meeting or slightly after, did you follow up with Jayne or anyone else on the team after communicating the disruptive change? Have you asked these questions?

- Are you ok with this change?
- Do you agree with this change?
- Are you onboard and will support this change?
- Do you have any further questions or want to talk about this change?
- Do you need help in communicating this change?

As a sales leader, why should you take the time to ask these questions? One might say to themselves, "I don't have that much time in the day to ask every salesperson if they are onboard with every change that we make during the week." If that is something you might say, then I ask you these questions: How do you know if the people held in your care to manage, and lead, agree with the changes you impose? Are you simply assuming that they will comfortably agree with every change decision you implement? And even if they will do it, are they onboard with it? Who are your change adopters? Who are your change deniers? How do you know if the sales team are going to actively support your direction? Did you give them the chance or opportunity to speak, to challenge a decision, or to possibly suggest an even better proposition? Who on your team is truly happy with your leadership decisions and who is a flight risk? Now, let's go back to Jayne. She is stuck trying to determine the best way to inform her accounts that their most popular promotional offer is now being withdrawn.

The gap between decision and action

Sitting at her desk, staring blankly into her computer screen, Jayne needs to reflect on the situation. She's likely asking herself, "How am I supposed to tell my accounts that the most successful promotional offer in our company's history is gone?" She's definitely viewing this change in a negative light, especially as no one gave her a choice or any ideas to help her communicate this to accounts. She is also frightened that she won't be able to hit her key performance indicators (KPIs) and sales targets without this promotional offer. The boss has just taken away her ability to sell and reach her quota, and gave her nothing to replace it. Jayne is lost. And feeling frustrated, she begins to draft an email to her accounts:

> Tom Orrow
>
> Director of National Accounts
>
> Rainy Day Supplies
>
> I regret to inform you that a decision was made today by our senior leadership to cease the current promotional offer we have had in place

for the current and past few quarters. At this time, I do not have any information on a replacement promotional offer for you to use with your clients and customers. I sincerely hope that this will not poorly reflect on our longstanding partnership. Effective immediately the terms and conditions including this offer are no longer available.

I must remind you that our current sales agreements and our quarterly sales quotas remain in effect at full pricing. Let us meet early next week to develop a plan to sell at full retail price without this promotional offer and see how we can continue to hit our mutual goals together.

Sincerely,

Jayne Simon

National Accounts Manager

Sunshine Umbrella Solutions

Before Jayne hits send, she reaches out to her sales leader to try and go over her communication to ensure she is accurate. Her sales leader is wrapped up in other meetings and their calendar is blocked for the remainder of the day. Jayne sits on this email communication and proceeds through the rest of her day, but she has left a message with her sales leaders receptionist to call her as soon as possible if there is any chance of meeting with her boss before the day is over. It is now 6 p.m. and Jayne hasn't heard back from the receptionist nor her sales leader. But the direction was that she was to notify her accounts immediately and that meant today. She calls her supervisor again and unfortunately gets the out-of-office response. What is Jayne to do? She hits send. Why did Jayne wait to send the email message? The message itself properly informs the account of the decision to pull the promotional offer. But it is also filled with an element of doom and gloom, and she's implied a disconnect between herself and her supervisors which could hurt the client's view of her company.

Imagine being the account customer and receiving that email. This change counters another change for the account customer that is going to receive it. If they are like most of us, they will receive that message on their mobile phone that evening and begin to fret and worry about how this change will affect them all night long until they can get in touch with Jayne the next day.

In this gap between decision and action, Jayne did take an action and drafted the email communication. However, she sat on it for a while and tried to have a further discussion with her sales leader about it but could not get through. Was Jayne a change adaptor? Was she a change detractor? She did what she was told to do and facilitated the change. But could it have been in a more informed and positive manner? Could there have been a dialogue with the sales leader and perhaps the other sales team members? What if a variation of the promotional offer could be reached or agreed to rather than just removing it all at once? Could there have been a different array of outcomes? The answer is yes.

Indeed, many actions could have been taken between the sales leaders and with Jayne and the sales team. Even direction on how to communicate this on a positive level would have been extremely helpful. How is Jayne feeling about her job and the safety and security of her ability to make money and reach her own targets as she leaves for the day? Probably not that great. In fact, based on the tone of the email she sent, it sounds like Jayne is up for a night of worrying about her sales future and her own role.

This is only one small scenario; these things can come up a few times a week at Jayne's level. How people perceive change becomes real and has physical and emotional outcomes that can immediately begin to effect one's thinking and sense of wellbeing. Jayne's gap between decision and action came and went. She tried to seek clarity or support from her sales leader but was unable to in time. At the end of the day, she had to follow the direction given, which was to communicate this change to her accounts.

There are a wide array of options or opportunities that Jayne could have written or communicated with her account manager on this situation. By using SCARED, Jayne could have stopped and talked herself through the change scenario and took actions towards making an informed decision that she would feel better about. She then could have used SO WHAT to create action points to support her strategy and take ownership of the situation. The outcomes could have led her to call her account customer and notify them in advance that an email was coming but that they would get together shortly to make a plan of action together. Her actions could have guided her to write the email in a more favorable manner so as to not cause concern or confusion. What she wrote was not bad, but it could have been more favorable, such as in the next example:

Tom Orrow

Director of National Accounts

Rainy Day Supplies

Hello Tom, I need to let you know that we have a change to our existing promotional offer you are currently sharing with your customers. This longstanding offer has to come to a close effective immediately. As of today, we need to go back to offering your customers our umbrellas at full retail price.

I don't want you to worry about this. Upon opening tomorrow you'll need to remove the offer and put the umbrella products back at full retail. But I want to visit with you and my sales supervisor soon, and together we will come up with a new plan to maximize our profits while meeting the needs of our customers. Please give me a call or email me back to set up a time to discuss our pricing and promotional plans for the rest of the quarter.

The forecast is for lots of rain the next few weeks. Full price for a little bit will benefit us both. We will make a plan together. I look forward to talking with you shortly.

Sincerely,

Jayne Simon

National Accounts Manager

Sunshine Umbrella Solutions

While it is easy to suggest a different way of communicating, the reality is that Jayne was stuck between the decision made for her to cancel the offer and her own decision to act by sending the email. She wanted to have more information or a discussion with her sales leader, but they were not available. As Jayne was feeling poorly about the decision, she reflected this in her communication and went home presumably feeling negative about the entire situation. Now this is a simple example of how changes and decisions made from a sales meeting can affect a salesperson. One might say many things about how Jayne responded or how she or her team members could have reacted to the meeting. And, truth be told, there are quite a few action items that could have happened from both the sales leader and the sales team in this situation. For example:

SALES LEADER RESPONSE

- Effective immediately the current promotions are cancelled.

- Email your accounts and inform them. Keep the message positive.

- Assure them that we will revisit with new promotional offers shortly.

- The next few weeks are forecasted for heavy rain—putting our products at full retail will ensure a higher profit margin for your accounts and the company.

- You will still earn your commissions and possibly more due to supply/ demand with the rainy season coming.

- Is everyone onboard with this? Any further questions or concerns?

SALES REPRESENTATIVES RESPONSE

- Should we meet as a sales team to create an email template message to be on the same page?

- Do we have any questions or concerns to share before the meeting ends?

- Can we call our accounts and give them a heads up?

- Do we all support this change? Is anyone unsure?

The gap between decision and action often leaves too much room for interpretation. In this example, Jayne was missing information she needed to fully understand the actions and consequences of terminating the promotional offer. While this may seem trivial, what if Jayne was a new hire sales member? She might not have the wealth of experience to know what could possibly come later when the sales leadership meets at the next revenue and or trading meeting. Or perhaps Jayne was very experienced, and she knew too well that the company would abruptly stop and start promotional offers and lacked in communicating the outcomes for sales members and their ability to earn commissions. No matter how trivial the example given, this is something that happens within the sales community and so many more changes of greater significance occur as well. People often tend to be in a state of flux or even confusion, a pause, or a hesitancy to act after a change situation has occurred. They might not immediately have the answers or information necessary to continue onward to the action stage and make the right choices.

As sales leaders, it is our role to work proactively instead of just simply acting transactionally. The example given was a demonstration of a tick-box exercise. The sales leader during a meeting informed the team to terminate a promotional offer and send via written email communication immediately and then closed the meeting. That is an example of leading transactionally. The leader told them to perform an action without providing meaning behind the action. However, a proactive and transformational leader would not only facilitate the direction, but then they would stick with the team to ensure they were fully informed about the reason for the decision and provide guidance and support and ensure the members are all onboard before closing the meeting. There is much evidence in today's modern literature about leadership and how to work in a transformational leadership style that is more conducive to enhanced employee development, performance, and wellbeing. I strongly encourage you to read up on this topic as a way of leading yourself and your team members. A transformational leader will work to close that gap between decision and action. A transactional leader most likely will not. The outcomes of that leadership style can be immensely different. Which way do you prefer to lead? And by the same token, as a sales professional, which way do you want to work?

How to make an informed decision and then confront change

How do we bridge and/or close the gap between making an informed decision about a personal change situation to performing actions based upon those decisions? The first and most important element is to ensure that we are making informed decisions.

In the case of Jayne, she had to communicate a less than favorable message to her accounts. Her email came after a decision made without her and she was instructed to act on it. She still questioned the intent, design, and delivery, as well as the outcome of that decision and what it meant for her and her clients. She was unable to collect further information, so went onward to execute the actions she was directed to do. Jayne did what she was told, but this left her with confusion and anxiety as well as the customer receiving the message. Herein lies the problem with much of the leadership and employee relationship we find happening in today's business world. The lack of information can cause this gap between decision and action to occur. Typically, our front-line salespeople do not know the full story behind leadership drives or actions and plans. Therefore, they are often left to make their own assumptive decisions without clarity of knowledge. One could argue that they could have better outcomes if they were able to make an informed decision with all the facts after having their questions answered. This could also lead to better employee performance and sales performance.

We need to begin with the sales employees and sales leadership themselves. The leaders must recognize that change is personal. How change is introduced in the work environment should incorporate the concerns of the individuals expected to carry out and execute those corporate change directives. Change is personal. It is constant and how we manage it can make it bearable and achievable for all those involved. Likewise, the sales members need to also learn how to manage personal change for themselves. SCARED SO WHAT is a methodology that can lead credibility, ease, and peace of mind for both sales leaders and salespeople together on change journeys.

A decision has been made

Now that a decision has been made it is time for you to move on to the next phase in executing a change process. If you reflect back on the change models that we have uncovered within this book, most of them do not have a guide or a next step at the end of the model. SCARED focuses on the feeling side of personal change. It invites you to learn how to stop and critically reflect on the change situation you find yourself within. Think about this change and ask yourself the questions that represent each letter in SCARED. The key to making an informed decision is in the actions you employ to generate information. This happens in two phases. The first is Action, where you ask questions to seek information. Then you might begin to formulate your response emotion of either being receptive or rejective of the change. And that also includes the possibility of being somewhat neutral to the change. It really depends on the change occurring itself. But the second action is Explore, which is a second chance to explore further options or opportunities to generate information for you to review about the change. From there, you should have enough information to make an informed decision regardless of whether it is favorable or unfavorable. Everyone's situation will be unique to them. From there, having made an informed decision you will then need to move to an action point in order to effectively transition through the change process occurring. This is where you bridge and close that gap between decision to action.

In our earlier example, Jayne was confronted with new information about a favored promotional offer—that it must end immediately. She needed more information and was forced to make a negative decision that led to an action being achieved. She followed the direction of her sales leader. But there could have been a more favorable outcome for both Jayne and for the customer that would have relieved unnecessary stress and anxiety on both parts. This is a perfect example of how a lack of information can lead to the job getting done, but it could have had different outcomes to benefit all members.

So, what?

Transitioning from a decision to an action can occur by making an informed decision with SCARED, and then moving on to making your own action plan with SO WHAT. Sir Isaac Newton's third law of motion states that for every action there is an opposite and equal reaction (Lucas, 2022). I relate this also to making and executing on a decision. Once a decision is made, regardless of whether it is favorable or unfavorable, an action or outcome must occur if that decision is to be acted upon. Simply meaning, just because a decision is made, does not necessarily mean that decision will become reality. Another force must happen to make that decision a reality. For example, let's say Jayne decided that she is going to sell $50,000 in quota this month even though her supervisor has eliminated the promotional offer. Great! She's made a decision on a goal. But how is she going to turn that into a reality? To achieve this, she is going to need her own plan of action.

And that is where SO WHAT comes into play. SO WHAT is the output of an informed decision made during the SCARED reflective process. It is the making of your own plan of action to support the outcome of the decision made. But what are you going to do about it? In Jayne's case, the company has decided to stop this offer, and it's up to the sales reps to determine what to do about it. When a change occurs, something needs to be done to reflect the change in practice or as it applies in the real world. (If a change occurs and nothing changes, then did anything really happen?)

Very few business plans or decisions are made without having a strategy plan to support the desired outcomes. When managing personal change, we do not have to simply sit idly by and hope that the changes we find ourselves within are magically going to work themselves out. We too can have our own brainstorming sessions to help us make informed decisions. We can use the SCARED process of asking questions to help us become more informed. We can thereby make our own strategy and set a plan to help us react to the situation and move from it.

Conclusion

SCARED SO WHAT is a tool and a learnable skillset for critical reflective thinking about personal change. When you find yourself in a situation where you are feeling nervous, anxious, stressed, or frustrated, and are not sure what to do about a change situation that you are experiencing, don't just ask others what you are supposed to do. Take control over the change and close that gap between decision and action for yourself. By thinking and asking yourself a few honest questions, you clearly gain valuable insight on how a personal change situation is happening or occurring with you. The key is to never make an assumption based on lack of information, especially when your instincts are telling you differently. By asking questions, we gain data points to help us review and consider. Doing this can lead us to making the right decisions and avoid that pondering self-questioning that typically occurs and leads us towards wasting precious time. Until now, we have not been taught how to think or reflect on personal change. SCARED helps us to do just that. And once we have made an informed decision, then it is time for us to make our own SO WHAT plan of action to execute the changes we are facing.

As sales members, we are faced with countless situations of change each and every day. Changes in the form of KPIs, quota requirements, sales targets, pipeline generation, promotional offers, and sales tools. We are also faced with being the brokers between the business customer, our organization, and the end customers that we are hoping to sell our overall products and services to. Change received from sales and contract rejections, to changes of terms and agreements and marketing and promotional opportunities, or lack thereof. Yet somehow, as sales professionals we are always supposed to be positive, upbeat, and maintain that can-do attitude and spirit. We are a different breed of working professionals, that I agree with. But we can be much more successful if we learn how to manage changes that become very personal by making informed decisions and creating our own SO WHAT. In the next chapter, we will learn how to do just that. We will break down into full detail that next piece, called SO WHAT. In other words, a change has occurred—so, what? What happens now? We'll go through creating an action plan to help you manage your team during tough times.

Before we do move to the next chapter, I would like to suggest some of my favorite authors for you to read in furthering your leadership development. If you are willing to grow your own leadership style, I would suggest reading further on *Leading Transformationally* through these authors' works. There are many more great examples to help you to enrich your leadership style, but these are some of my personal must-read choices on this subject and I hope you enjoy them as much as I do:

- *Everyday People, Extraordinary Leadership: How to make a difference regardless of your title, role or authority* (Kouzes and Posner, 2021)

- *The Motive: Why so many leaders abdicate their most important responsibilities* (Lencioni, 2020)

- *Contemporary Leadership Theories, Enhancing the understanding of the complexity, subjectivity, and dynamic of leadership* (Winkler, 2010)

- *Everyone Communicates, Few Connect: What the most effective people do differently* (Maxwell, 2010)

- *Good to Great: Why some companies make the leap ... and others don't* (Collins, 2001)

08

Creating a SO WHAT plan

As a sales and business leader, you need to determine the best way to support your team members through the variable aspects of change that involves the sales employees under your direction and responsibility. It is critical for your sales team to be onboard with the changes you and others are making in order to achieve your organizational goals and key performance indicators of success. Not only do you need to support them, but you need to make sure that the changes imposed do not negatively impact the work they're doing to drive performance success. By now you should have a better understanding that SCARED SO WHAT as a method of managing personal change does not mean that you or your sales team members literally have to be scared in order to use it. As I have illustrated in prior chapters, the model works for all types of change situations no matter if they are positive, neutral, or negative. One thing that is very common is that once a change scenario is presented, the first reaction you or your sales team might have is a feeling of, "OK, so what does that mean to me?" (Or, more accurately, "So, what?") This piece is where most of the organizational change models that we have talked about drop off. So, what happens to the individual who is expected to do something about—and often carry out and execute—the change? The SO WHAT piece aims to help those impacted by change to act on it (after they've made sense of it in "SCARED"). This is an opportunity for you as a sales leader to help your colleagues critically reflect on the changes happening to them and with them, and then help them to learn how to make an action plan to manage it for themselves.

SO WHAT: what do I do about it?

Once you have made an informed decision then it should be time to consider how you are going to manage or execute your personal change process. Every change scenario is different, and some situations are more complex than others. But let us take a deeper look at the SO WHAT model and determine the best ways to utilize it and when (see Figure 8.1, which you should recognise from Chapter 5).

The hardest part about managing personal change is knowing where to begin. Taking an informed decision and then building upon that decision in a well-thought-out and planned structure can only support you in building your own version of change success. That begins with building your strategy of how you are going to manage the change process. While we have provided some guiding points on what could be included in each section of the SO WHAT model, I would like to go a little bit deeper with each area to bring focus and attention for you to consider. Let us begin by taking a deeper look at what we mean by the first piece of SO WHAT: *Strategy*.

FIGURE 8.1 SO WHAT Wheel to Navigate Change

Strategy

What is a strategy? What does it mean to me within a business setting? Better yet, what does it mean to me within a personal setting? Henry Mintzberg (1987) defines a strategy as a "consciously intended course of action, a guideline (or set of guidelines) to deal with a situation". A simple example could be making a plan of how you are going to make a sales presentation. What are the steps involved to get you there? What tools or preparation would you need to consider? Do you need to have a slide presentation, or will the sales numbers suffice? Thinking through how you are going to facilitate an action is a form of strategy making. Mintzberg further states that the facility of making a strategy includes two characteristics. The first one being that they are made in advance of the actions of an event or a situation that needs to take place. The second one is that they are developed consciously and purposefully. This means that you have put thought into the actions you are wanting to occur, and you willfully made these actions that formulate your strategy.

For a personal change scenario, you should want to put some thought into the actions you are going to take to act upon the change. This is the first characteristic of Mintzberg's definition of a strategy. You reflect upon what actions you could take in advance before acting upon those plans you have made. Next, you should strive to put some thought into it and make a conscious effort with full intention or purpose. Therefore, by applying the definition, the making of a strategy or strategic plan can benefit you and apply to a personal change situation as well.

Next, you might be saying, "What do I include in my personal strategy plan?" And that is a great question. Since the change you are going through is unique to your own situation as a salesperson, there are a few options on how you might begin building your personal strategy. You can do this process either by yourself or enlist the support of a sales colleague or supervisor. You do not have to make your strategy all on your own. You might want to take the first approach so that you are able to articulate your own thoughts and potential action items. But including others afterwards is a smart decision for follow-up and support. The starting point from there is to identify and clarify what the change itself is to you. What is the change that you are experiencing? Can you name it? If so, write it down. You can do this in a notebook, on a blank sheet of paper, in a computer, or even on a whiteboard. Whatever is easy for you to begin documenting your own strategy plan. Once you are able to identify what the change is itself, then you want to ensure that you are including what the items of concern may be. Ask yourself, "What are my key objectives?" List out what you want to happen as a result of this change. Next, begin to document what steps you need to take within the change process. Is it all happening at the same time or will there be little changes that happen over a period of time? Focus on identifying what it is that you need to do as part of your action plan to initiate or accept the change.

As you begin to capture these important elements, start to think about what processes may be involved with your change plan. Are there any other people that need to be informed or notified of potential actions you will be taking as a result of your change situation? Don't forget to focus on your own needs as well. Try to identify what constraints or obstacles you might experience as a result of launching your action plan or strategy. The more you can detail for yourself the more prepared you will be in managing your change successfully. Other important items that you may wish to consider include budgetary constraints, systems and tools for support, time and time management, and other people that may be needed to help action your change plan. Once you have determined all of the factors that need to be a part of your change strategy, then you will also wish to consider potential timelines and dates of when you want this change to be completed by. Ask yourself this question: "When do I want to complete this change plan?"

Options

To complement your strategy and ensure that it is as thorough as it can be, you will want to step back from creating your strategy plan and then to reflect. Determine if there are there any other relevant Options or Opportunities to include in the strategy plan. "Option" is a word that dates back to the 1600s and means the "actions to choose" (Etymonline, 2020). It is here that we are asking you to critically reflect and think about any other actions you might want to choose to become a part of your strategy plan. If you cannot think of any, then you might wish to ask others for their feedback, or you could be on the right track. There is nothing wrong with asking other people or stakeholders for their opinions or suggestions about the plan you are making. It actually shows vulnerability and confidence in sharing your work with others as a way to ensure that your plan is the best it can possibly be. This is especially true if your strategy plan involves others to help you enact or execute the change that you find yourself within. Once you feel confident that you have a strong strategy in place, then you can move onto the next step.

Way forward

The Way forward phase of your self-reflection is a moment for you to review your strategy and ask yourself the following questions:

- Have I identified who I might need to include to review my plan or provide me with support?
- Have I identified all the stakeholders that will be involved with my strategy and plan?
- Do I need to bring anyone else onboard before I'm ready to enact or continue with my change decision?

In essence, what you are stopping and asking yourself at this moment is, "Do I feel comfortable with my strategy plan?" You are looking to be able to say, "Yes, I see a way forward with this plan." In doing so, you are able to reassure yourself that you have given your strategy plan the right amount of due diligence necessary to be effective. The next question that comes will challenge if you are able to execute your strategy plan.

Hope/how

Hope or *how* is the step where you are now able to fact-check and question if your plan is relevant and if there are any holes or missing items that you have not yet thought about. This is a pause for you to conduct a second review. Do not think of it as second guessing your work. It is always a good process to implement before rushing into a plan of action. You want to be certain that you have put the proper time and energy into your plan of actions. At this time, you will want to begin asking yourself the following questions:

- Do I have the right plan in place?
- Do I have others' buy in and support or are they still stuck in indecision?
- Do I have the leadership support or approvals necessary for my strategy and options?

If you can answer yes for all three questions, then you are ready to move forward and enact your strategic plan for managing your own personal change situation or scenario. However, if you answer no or you are unsure, then this would be the proper time to go back and begin reviewing what your options or opportunities you have uncovered and what the bulk items of your strategic plan include. This will save you valuable time and energy in the future if you need to stop now and reconsider your action plan. Now that you have your plan well established and are feeling confident that it will work, the next item that you need to consider are the actions you will take to ensure your plan goes smoothly.

Actions

If you thought that you were finished just because you made a strong strategy plan... I would hope you know better! But in the event you don't know it, that's why you are here—to read and learn how to make the most for your personal change management success. In sales and business, many strategy plans are just the beginning steps.

It is the foundation of what you are going to do or achieve. And there is no difference when it comes to managing personal change. In this phase you want to begin to think about launching or enacting your plan to support change. Here, you are thinking to yourself, "What actions do I need to take to ensure that my strategy goes off as smoothly as I have planned for it to?" That is a very important item to consider. In answering that question you want to begin to list those items down. List out any names of potential stakeholders that you need to involve or ask for support or approval. Start to reflect on any timelines that you need to put into place for your strategy plan to begin or take shape. Set deadlines and goals for yourself so that you know how to manage your time and actions. What milestones will you stop and celebrate? What does success look like for you? Do you have key performance indicators or targets that you want to achieve? If yes, write them all down. These become the *action* items that you will use and drive towards in executing your strategic plan.

Take ownership

Taking ownership is the ability to assign responsibility to one's own self rather than expecting others to take action or accountability. It is 100 percent about you taking charge of your own actions and behavior, ensuring that you are taking into account everything you need to do and achieve. Aside from creating a well-thought-out strategy plan for combating or managing personal change, taking ownership is most likely the key ingredient to seeing your change plans come to fruition. Within your action plan, you should be documenting all of these steps with action items and bullet points about the contents of your plan. It is here, in the taking ownership portion, that you will want to ask yourself these important questions and document their answers:

- How will I hold myself accountable to execute my personal change plan?
- Who will I share my plan with and communicate so that I can be successful?

- Who will be my key stakeholders to check in with for support if needed?
- How will I know that progress is made and how will I report or share that?
- Will I check with others involved in my plan to ensure they have what they need? (Could be just with yourself—stop and reflect.)
- How will I see my plan through, and will I ask anyone for help if needed? Who would I ask?
- How will I celebrate any successes or regroup if necessary to support towards success?

Let's break this down a bit further so you can be sure to understand the importance of what each question is asking: "How will I hold myself accountable...?" Here in this question your answers should include the steps or stages necessary within your action plan. Which step will you achieve first and by when and what date and time? Give yourself the opportunity to create stages that you can mark complete and say, "That's done!" That is one way you can ensure you will hold yourself accountable. Knowing who you will share your plan with and being able to gain their sign off is another actionable item that you can help to add clarity if your plans are on the right track or not. Who needs to know about it? Then check them off the list once they have been made aware. This also goes hand-in-hand with knowing who your stakeholders will be. Each of them should have a responsibility even if it is just being aware of what is being done or required of them or people under their care.

Next you will want to ask yourself, "How will I know that progress is made...?" That depends on your change process. If you are changing jobs due to an organizational change announcement, how will you know when progress is made? Maybe it is when you have your first one-to-one review with your new leader in your new position. Perhaps it is once you finish your first month in that new role. Whatever it is, it will be unique to you. Try to document these types of milestones so that you know when to look for success and can be able to identify what success means to you. After all, this is about managing personal change and that means it is personal. If there are other people or stakeholders involved within your strategy plan, will you check in with them during the change process? If yes, when will you do that? How will you do it? Email, in person, or virtual call? Make sure you are thinking through about these action items and milestones, because by creating awareness now you are setting yourself up for greater success of your plan in the future. And, most importantly, do not be afraid to ask for help or guidance from others along the way. This could be from a colleague or a stakeholder that you have identified as a person to go to for help or guidance.

How do I create my own SO WHAT strategy plan?

If you are like me, I love using templates. But then again, some people like to create their own from scratch. There really is no right or wrong. In many business settings, the strategy plan document itself is typically made up in a PowerPoint presentation document. Behind that document are all of the supporting mechanisms like Excel files, Power BI files, Sales Force files, and so forth. But for us to create a personal change management strategy plan, maybe a template is a good place to start for the first time. As such, there is a SO WHAT template (see Appendix 1) that we have made freely available for you to download from our website. I'll show you where to get this towards the end of the book. But right now, let me walk you through it here in detail for each area of the SO WHAT template.

For this example, let us focus on our salesperson, Jayne, from Chapter 7 and her change scenario that occurred when her managers informed her and the team to immediately discontinue a long-standing sales promotion for their accounts. They had to do this on the day they were informed. In this scenario, if you recall, Jayne has made a negative decision as she was not feeling good about this. Nevertheless, she has made a decision and now needs to move forward to strategically think this through by building her own SO WHAT.

In the first example (Table 8.1), the probing action items are in the left-hand column. Jayne has answered each of the column guiding points with her input on the right-hand side to formulate her change Strategy.

TABLE 8.1 Jayne's Strategy

The sorts of things to consider when building a STRATEGY	The items that Jayne is considering to include in her STRATEGY
Identifying and clarifying the change	End of promotional offer: communicate to accounts effective today (immediately)
Steps to include in the change	Discuss with team members messaging Align on announcement timing Draft communication Ensure reinforcement and ask to meet shortly Be available for immediate feedback/support
Processes and people that need to be involved	Sales team—alignment Accounts involved Supervisor in copy Marketing for potential full retail collateral needs Sales support and call center for service needs
Needs/constraints/support mechanisms/budget	Alignment from sales team members Timing is tight Ensure support is available for questions and feedback from accounts
Tools necessary	Sales collateral to switch from promotion to full price, salesforce, email
Timelines	Accounts messaging by 5pm Sales service and marketing support by 4pm
Communication process	Email with a meeting request for follow up

This is Jayne's Strategy plan. If you are like me, you may be seeing some other items that could be added. There are other things that could be considered but, again, in this scenario Jayne is not happy about this change. She is worried about her ability to make her targets. However, she is doing what she was told to do. And creating this action plan helps to ensure she can complete the actions necessary.

The next step for Jayne to review is to see if there are any other options or opportunities that would support her plan (Table 8.2).

TABLE 8.2 Jayne's Options

The sorts of things to consider when building OPTIONS	The items that Jayne is considering to include in her OPTIONS
Identifying other options and opportunities	Is there another offer that will be coming soon? Do we know how long this offer will be rescinded? Is there a positive aspect to this situation where everyone wins?
People and processes necessary to support your plan—fact and sense check the plan	Sales team members My sales supervisor The account customer
Workshops may be necessary (small or large) for idea generation/collaboration	Sales team to go back to supervisor Maybe include revenue management
Support needed/Processes and people	Sales team, immediate supervisor, and account manager from customer side

From here, there is a second approach to formulating the strategy plan. Remembering that Jayne was not happy about the direction, you can see that she is beginning to question if there are other possible opportunities. Is there another offer that will be coming from her sales leader and or revenue management in the near future that might help her and the other sales team members to draft their communications to their accounts? If there is another alternative, then why not communicate it? And most importantly, she has identified that she needs to include her counterpart account manager with her customer. They too may have insights or ideas on what can be achieved simply by working together. This is the reason Options and Opportunities is here. It is a chance to review or consider further options you might not have considered before you act or react.

Jayne is ready to move on with her strategy making process to assess her own Way forward. Here is the opportunity for her to reflect before she takes actions. Let us look at this example together (Table 8.3).

TABLE 8.3 Jayne's Way forward

The sorts of things to consider when assessing a WAY FORWARD	The items that Jayne is considering including in assessing her WAY FORWARD
Identifying who will need to be in the Review/Approval process	If there is to be another offer, then revenue management, my supervisor. Today I do not need approval to send the communication. I'm ok to send
Identifying key stakeholders—blockers and/or supporters	My counterpart at Rainy Day Supplies may not be happy. But my supervisor has directed me to do this
Are workshops needed?	Not at this time
Support person or items?	Sales team, service and marketing notification

TABLE 8.4 Jayne's Hope/How

The sorts of things to consider when reflecting on HOPE/HOW	The items that Jayne is considering in her reflection on HOPE/HOW
Do I have the right plan in place?	I'm not comfortable with the direction but I do have other options/opportunities that I can explore later. My plan for today is accurate and workable
Do I have the teams buy in and support or are they stuck in indecision?	The sales team are feeling the same. But they have moved onto Decision
Do I have the leadership support/approval of my Strategic plan and Way Forward?	Yes, for discontinuing the offer. No for future options but we must follow their direction for today
If I'm missing any of the above, I may need to revisit the Strategy and Options and recalculate my Way forward	Want to revisit the options with my team and supervisor post today's notification
If I am ok with the above, then I can move forward	Must send for now

Jayne has decided that she can move forward because she has to do what her supervisor has instructed. But already you can see that she is questioning to see if there are other offers that could potentially become available. She is trying to plan ahead for how she is going to reach her own targets. Rightfully so, she is concerned. But she can move forward. Her next step is a moment to pause and ask if she knows How she will achieve this change directive or have Hope that her plan is correct (Table 8.4).

Just from Jayne's writing on Hope/How you can begin to see where her mind is at. She is not happy about it but she will rightfully follow the direction of her supervisor. However, she has some options and a plan for discussing them with her team and supervisor after sending out the communication today. The next questions surround the Actions she will take to execute her strategy (Table 8.5).

TABLE 8.5 Jayne's Actions

The sorts of things to consider when considering ACTIONS to take	The items that Jayne is considering in her ACTIONS to take
Actions to launch your plan should have been identified and included in your strategy and options section. Itemize them here	Discuss with team members messaging Align on announcement timing Draft communication Ensure reinforcement and ask to meet shortly Be available for immediate feedback/ support
Who do you need to help take this plan forward?	Align with sales team on messaging
Begin your plan to include	Sales team alignment—then email accounts
Leadership support to launch	Sales supervisor already provided direction
Communication process	Email follow up by phone next day
Implementation process	Start the same time as other sales members
Key performance measures or indicators	Email feedback at this moment. Sales volume/results
Timelines	Today for comms/Tomorrow for follow up with customer. Tomorrow for supervisor about other options

TABLE 8.6 Jayne's Taking ownership

The sorts of things to consider when reflecting on how to TAKE OWNERSHIP	The items that Jayne is considering including to ensure she TAKES OWNERSHIP
Holding myself accountable—how?	1st: Send the initial email 2nd: Communicate with supervisor and team next day about potential other offers or suggestions 3rd: Follow up with sales team and customer and continue support
Sharing and communicating your vision	Will do the above with sales team, customer, and supervisor
Checking and supporting the implementation to leaders	Will copy supervisor on outgoing email to customers
Reporting out progress	As above and will also share feedback from customer/teams
Support of those involved	Supervisor, customer, sales team, sales and service support, revenue management
Checking in with people involved to ensure they have what is necessary (can just be with yourself)	Will check in tomorrow with all, will continue follow up throughout offer removal timeframe
Seeing your plan through and asking for help when necessary	Meeting scheduled for tomorrow with team, customer and supervisor
Celebrate success and/or regroup if necessary to bring people back into supporting success	Pending at this time. Will circle back as needed

As you can see, Jayne is taking action by working her strategic plan through. She has already identified other options and opportunities, and now she is creating the action items not only to support her customers but also her other team members, and her own plan to support her own revenue generation and earning power to achieve targets but also that of her team members. This is the level of detail behind her change process. Without this level of critical thinking, she might have just sent the email in a negative tone and done nothing else about it. This could cause further stress and anxiety for her but also for her customers. Jayne has formulated other action points through this process. But there is one more final step and that is to ensure that Jayne Takes ownership (Table 8.6).

By now Jayne has created her own SO WHAT action and strategy plan for managing her situation of personal change. It is personal to her because it involves a change in her ability to generate her own key performance indicators and reach her sales targets. She perceives that this will be the case. And perception is Jayne's reality as it would be for anyone involved in this situation. Early on in Chapter 7, we saw how Jayne responded to her change situation, and we saw how that communication could have been more positive. In this chapter, we have seen what could have happened had Jayne used the SO WHAT plan of action to create her own strategy. In doing so, Jayne has clearly seen that there are other options or opportunities for her to uncover and explore. She followed through on the direction provided by her supervisor but now she is able to go home feeling a little bit better. Perhaps she feels she has more of a sense of control now that she has a plan that includes questioning other potential outcomes. This gives Jayne a better sense of hope and confidence in a possible different outcome that can benefit her as she moves forward.

Conclusion

To avoid rushing to conclusions or jumping into action as a form of reaction, we are suggesting that you slow down and reflect upon the change head on. Think it through and make an informed decision. From there, you can begin to build your own SO WHAT strategy template. We know this process works, because building strategies within the common business community is a global standard practice. Therefore, what we are suggesting is to build one for your own sense of self as well. Remember, the change is personal… What are you going to do about it? Create your own SO WHAT.

The example we provided was a typical example of a change communication in a sales environment where a promotional offer has to be withdrawn. One might think that this is very simple and that any salesperson overthinking this would be absurd. But I question that line of thinking and really poor example of leadership. Any change made in the work environment and sales arena is an action.

And as Sir Isaac Newton has theorized, an action has to have an equal and opposite effect or reaction. Salespeople are no different. Whenever we as sales leaders start to take away or influence the ability of our salespeople to reach their quotas or sales targets and key performance indicators, we must realize that our actions might have an effect on their ability to earn sales commissions and payroll. This is the consequence of our actions. Even the seasoned sales veteran is probably going to have a reaction to anything that touches their ability to earn their sales commissions. Something so small as removing a promotion without any further communication or plan of what is coming next can cause an entire sales team to immediately go into question and concern mode. This example, however small it may seem, has the ability to cause a significant effect on their livelihoods, at least for that day or week—until further communication and or direction comes available.

The example provided and shared is the use of a template. This is recommended for whatever your change scenario is for the first time and perhaps even the second. But as you manage your way through and become more familiar with using and understanding the terminology and methodology, then it can become a practice of habit or a learnt skillset. You could even use the acronym SCARED SO WHAT on a piece of paper, a whiteboard, in a document or spreadsheet, or wherever you feel comfortable. The key is to learn this as a method of supporting your own ability to critically reflect on your thoughts and feelings and then into making a strategy plan for yourself. For large, impactful changes I would strongly recommend some sort of a template or process to create your own strategy plan. Big changes often need more people to be involved and participate. Writing the SO WHAT down and creating either your own SO WHAT or even a team-based SO WHAT can be very beneficial in creating alignment, camaraderie, and team support. What do you think? Could you create your own SO WHAT?

09

What's next?

So, what is next? What can a sales leader or salesperson do with SO WHAT on a daily basis within their work and practice? Is it as simple as taking some time, reflecting on what they may be going through during a change process and then documenting down a plan? Do I have to use the SO WHAT template every time? What about the SCARED quiz? Should I take that with every change situation that happens to me? Change is already complicated enough, one might say. Learning and beginning to use a new model requires practice and time and is in itself another change process. Right now, you might be saying to yourself that you understand the model and the principles behind it, but you're unsure if you can really use it. A sales leader might think this to be clunky or difficult to get others to utilize. But with any new change, practice is required if we are going to eventually master it. Learning a new model is no different, but I assure you that you can do it. And very quickly both you and your sales team members can see how it can become a common practice and a new skillset or way of thinking about managing personal change. With any strategy plan, an element of flexibility must be included. We learn as we grow, and we enhance our strategic plans as we gain new experiences and learn new things. Let us look at how SO WHAT needs to be and can be flexible.

Flexing your own SO WHAT

As sales professionals, our jobs are typically fast-paced, action-oriented, and probably a bit hectic in order to drive the sales performance necessary if we are going to reach our quota and sales targets. That is the nature of the sales game. We have been conditioned over decades of learning and experiences with hand-me-down outdated tips and tricks branded as "consultative sales techniques" for how we can manipulate and close the sale. But in today's reality, we need to realize that times change, and we are all human. As humans, we experience constant bouts of change. Change initiates emotions and emotions drive actions. And as we learnt in Chapter 3, Dr. Julian Birkinshaw (2014) states that, since 2010, "We are living in an Emocracy." An emocracy is where both the customer and the salesperson have co-equal sources of competitive advantage. And in an emocracy, buying decisions are largely based on emotion rather than facts themselves. And that must be familiar to us all as we are all living in the world of advanced social media, digital media, and digital/virtual forms of selling. Birkinshaw further shows how nearly seven people are involved in the buying decisions within a business-to-business setting. This means that for all of us tasked with sales generation, we sometimes find ourselves trying to sell to all seven of these people involved rather than the days of old when it was nearly a one-to-one sales/buying experience.

The ability to be highly flexible is considered an advanced skillset within the sales profession and more than ever that skillset is being tested. Think about the sales process we typically work within today. Whether it is before the sales interaction, during the sales interaction, or after the sales interaction, at every step a change curveball can come into play. Just like Jayne in our example with the cancellation of a longstanding promotional offer. Or maybe during a sales call, the customer flat out rejects the sales pitch in midstream. One could have had the best sales discussion ever and walk away thinking that deal was locked in and done. However, afterwards, the customer ghosted them and they've heard nothing back nor know why the customer is no longer responding. For opportunity managers, also known as business development managers, this type of rejection comes quite often.

Calling on potential customers and clients to gain and foster leads that can potentially generate a sale is an everyday task. And moreover, once they get the meeting and a chance to have a client interaction, they may or may not be talking to the right person out of the typical seven people necessary to make a buying decision within a business setting. Do they get any response? Perhaps the customer was no longer interested? And I would be remiss to leave out the sales development representatives who call and email, text, and use social media in trying to generate sales leads. They are constantly faced with rejection and/or no responses at all. A career in the sales profession includes constant rejection, changing of strategies, and changes to how the game is played on a daily basis. And those situations of change can take their toll on a person's conscience, confidence, and passion and ability to get up each day and keep going.

So how do we add flexibility in using creating and using our own SO WHAT? Some might be pleasantly surprised to know that it is relatively easy for one simple reason. The plan is yours and it is about you and your situation or experience with your own personal change. What does that mean? Think about a strategic plan at work. Typically, these plans take some time to make and are made with quite a few other people involved. Usually it is the sales leadership, accompanied by commercial managers and teams, supported with revenue management and perhaps even marketing and or operations. Together this team makes a strategy plan for how they are going to execute sales initiatives to meet the financial needs of the company. That requires a lot of effort and a team of leadership to sign off. For those seasoned in sales, this might sound familiar.

The difference with SO WHAT is that it is your plan for yourself. You have full control over what you put into your own SO WHAT plan. You have the freedom to share it with others and gain their feedback as you go, but you also have the freedom to change it by yourself as your change situation fluctuates or plays out over time. The other important thing to know is that you do not have to make it complex. If you have a big change situation happening such as an organizational structure change, job role change, moving to a new territory, adding or loss of promotional offers or sales tools, and even if your territory, call and customer volume, or market remit is increased or lowered, you might want to consider writing down and filling in your own SO WHAT change template. Large-scale changes that happen to you or with you might suit you better if you create a visual written or typed-up strategy. It gives you the opportunity to reflect on it and seek others' opinions or support so you can revise and edit it as you see fit.

The example with Jayne and losing the promotional offer really hit her hard. She was deeply concerned about her own ability to reach her sales targets and earn her commissions goals. Taking just a few minutes to write down her thoughts in a structured way allowed her to find other options and opportunities to discuss the topic with her sales team, her sales leader, and her customers. This allowed her to go home after delivering a hard message to her customer and reflect that she has options to pursue. What if she did not do the exercise? What do you think Jayne would have done that evening when she went home? You're right! She probably would have stressed the entire evening and into the next day because she had not thought about nor taken the time to reflect and draft other options or opportunities that could have been available. And that would have been an evening of unnecessary anxiety and tension.

Smaller changes are still forms of change, and they drive and affect our emotions. For example, a customer ghosting the salesperson and not calling them back. That hurts. It does! And for anyone who says it doesn't affect them, I would question if they were really telling the truth. Anytime we put forward our efforts and time to make a sales call and/or presentation to a potential client, that is an investment of ourselves. Having the client not call us back or, better yet, they do call us back, but reject our proposal, it is personal and takes a toll on our emotions. I would classify these as smaller change situations. They are important but perhaps they do not need the full written out SO WHAT plan. But the salesperson experiencing this situation still has an opportunity to learn from their efforts. And for this, they can think to themselves (reflection), "What went well?" "What didn't go well?" "What could I do differently?" and that is the start of an internal dialogue. This is the process of building their own Strategy, and thinking what other options or opportunities they could include. From there they move on continuing the self-conversation and ask, "Do I have a way forward now?" If yes, keep going. If no, then reflect again on the strategy and options. Maybe they need to ask for the help of a colleague and that would be great! It shows they are critically thinking their own personal change situation through. But if they can or when they can move forward, then before they move onto the next sales call or pitch, think to themselves, "Do I have Hope or know How I'm going to do this?" Next, they keep going onto what actions they would take and then think of how they could take ownership and hold themselves accountable to the strategy they have just created. SO WHAT can be done internally by having an internal conversation. The key to success is that salespeople utilizing this method are no longer just assuming or jumping to conclusions. They are making a concerted effort to critically reflect and build upon the change situation they are experiencing. A change situation can be an opportunity to learn something new.

Practice SCARED SO WHAT as you go

You've heard it before. People often say that practice makes perfect. If we are to do anything well, then yes, we need to practice at it. Until reading this book, you might have never even thought that you could actually learn to manage your own sense of personal change. And if you are reading this far in, it is probably because you are curious if this can really work for you. I believe it and know that it can as I have witnessed so many others in sales using this for themselves from all over the world. I made the SCARED SO WHAT model as a tool to lead my sales team members through transformation and change. I was inspired to create it because the leading models for managing organizational change made me feel that you as the individual had absolutely no say in a change situation at all. And I do not think that is true. As individuals, we have the ability and the right to accept change, just go along with change, and outright reject change. I wanted to create a model or a framework that would help you as the individual to be able to find your own voice within a change situation and be able to have help in managing it to your own personal situation and satisfaction. As I have articulated earlier on in this book, no one until now has taught us how to manage personal change. Our parents were not taught about it nor are the leading change management experts focusing on us as the individuals and how we manage change for ourselves. But now after creating this and sharing it with my sales members and even customers from Europe, the Middle East, and Africa, to Singapore, India, Malaysia, and throughout Australia and New Zealand, all the way throughout the United States, the Caribbean, Mexico, and the South American regions, people are learning how to manage personal change for themselves through SCARED SO WHAT. The effects and result are uniquely empowering! But... it takes practice.

Within our daily sales routine, change is going to happen. For that we can be certain. From small changes like customers not calling us back, flat out rejecting our sales presentations, to not being able to make quota or not earning enough commission, change will happen. And then to larger change situations like organizational restructures, job changes, market, and region switches, winning big deals, and even gaining a new promotion. No matter what the changes are that we find ourselves within, SCARED SO WHAT can be a methodology and a new skillset we can count on to add critical reflection into our sales practices.

As we have uncovered earlier, SCARED comes complete with a self-help quiz that you can take over and over again at any time. The same is true of SO WHAT, where you have a template that you can use to create your own detailed SO WHAT plan. These are tools that are available for you to use whenever you need. In the final chapter, I will share with you how these tools will evolve into the digital world to become easier for you to utilize. The tools are here now and readily available. Use them whenever you need. However, more importantly, SCARED SO WHAT can become a way of thinking in that you do not need to use the tools as they are but as a way of thinking. Let me share an example of how to do this.

Scenario A: SCARED SO WHAT

Sales agent: Shannon

THE SITUATION

Shannon has a sales quota to call on and or visit 50 potential solid lead clients in the month of June. These 50 potential solid lead clients are sourced from her assigned sales development representative (SDR). Out of those 50 potential clients, she needs to secure a 40 percent conversion ratio in generating new customers and business opportunities. History shows that with a 40 percent conversion ratio, that equates to 20 fresh customers that will typically generate the revenues necessary for the organization. Ok, simple enough right.

SHANNON'S REALITY

During the month, Shannon checks in with your SDR and she is confident that they will generate the 50 potential clients. To do this, they are calling out on 200 potential clients a day to find a solid client lead for her to then call on or visit and present her sales presentation. It is now June 25, and Shannon only has 12 clients converted. She needs eight more clients to hit her conversion quota, but she only has five more days in the month. This is a situation of personal and potentially stressful change. What does Shannon do? Many people will become very frustrated and start to make assumptions or accusations. Others will leave it up to chance. And yet others might simply say this is impossible.

Here is a perfect example of where Shannon could stop and critically reflect and think through the SCARED SO WHAT model. She doesn't need to stop and take the quiz, just think it through in her head for a few moments of internal dialogue with the best person to listen… herself! Follow through the internal discussion with Shannon:

> Am I **Surprised** by this situation? Yes, and it's not a good surprise as I'm most likely going to lose out on this month's commission.

Am I **Conflicted** about this? Absolutely yes, I am.

What **Actions** have I taken? None so far... perhaps I could call my SDR and try to find some fresh qualified leads. Or maybe I could double up my calling tomorrow and the next day and try to convert faster by phone or email or text. Maybe I could go to my supervisor and get a better deal to offer for these last few leads.... Ok there are still opportunities. Let me ask for some help.

Am I **Receptive** or **Rejective** of this? At first it was rejection, but now I have some other ideas so I'm a bit more receptive. Maybe I can pull this month's quota off and be ok.

Are there any other options I could **Explore**? Perhaps I could ask the other sales reps for advice? Bob is a colleague and friend; I'll ring him up now.

Have I made an informed **Decision**? Yes, feeling a bit more positive, I'm going to keep trying. At least I can give it my best shot.

So far so good. Shannon has started to reflect to herself using the SCARED process of critically reflecting on her situation. And during this, there are already some elements of a strategy coming to fruition. Let's continue the internal dialogue onto the SO WHAT portion.

Ok, so I'm good, I've made a decision. So, what can I do about it? Let's think this through. What's my **Strategy?** Well, I'm going to call Bob and seek his guidance on how sales are going and what he's doing to convert. I'm also going to reach out to my supervisor and ask for additional closing help. Maybe she has a closing bonus I can give to the client. Then tomorrow and the next day I'll double up my calls. I don't have time to go and visit every lead, so I'll stick by the phone and also email and text all leads to see if I can generate additional conversion. Good... I've got a plan.

Are there any other **Options** or opportunities? Wait, Jayne has already exceeded her quota, maybe she would be willing to help call on my behalf and I could help her with some commission share. Not a bad idea and within company guidelines.

> Do I have a **Way forward**? Yes, I think I do.
>
> Do I have **Hope** or know **How** I'm going to do this? Yes, I've got a plan. What **Actions** will I take to execute my plan? Let me write my plan and notes down now just to be sure.
>
> How will I **Take ownership**? I'm going to block my calendar tomorrow for client calls only. I'll schedule a call now with my supervisor. I'm going to call Jayne first thing in the morning—adding a meeting now at 8:30 am on the calendar with invite. I think this can work.

This situation is probably more common than one thinks, and is a real-life example but only the salesperson's name has been changed. While it may seem a small change, it quickly could have turned into a larger change situation if Shannon had not stopped to think, reflect, and make a plan of action. Like so many others, Shannon could have simply assumed that it was too late and that perhaps she was not going to make quota for the month. That assumption could have led her to actually not achieve her quota, which would have brought on an even greater change process because she would have potentially missed her commissions for the month. Missing commission earnings can lead to even greater change scenarios that I'm sure you can think of. What this exercise shows is that people do not have to use the tools or write things down every time for SCARED SO WHAT to help guide them in their thinking. For the big things, yes, perhaps one might want to and that even goes for positive changes like getting promoted or moving to a new sales region. Positive changes bring forth emotions and confusion as well. Stopping and taking some time to critically reflect using the SCARED SO WHAT methodology becomes a learned skillset that can stick with us for the rest of our lives. But what about those big changes—do I really need to use the SO WHAT template? Let us look at another, more serious, sales related change that might happen to us all one day.

Scenario B: SCARED SO WHAT

Sales agent: Shaun

THE SITUATION

Shaun has just come from a sales meeting where also in the meeting were a representative from human resources and the Senior Vice President of Sales. Normally, the sales meetings are led by the Vice President and/or Director of Sales. In this meeting, Shaun tries diligently not to read too much into why the human resources leader and the senior vice president are in attendance. The subject of the meeting is ORGANIZATIONAL RESTRUCTURE.

In this meeting, Shaun's vice president is leading the discussion and announces that, due to organizational needs, there is going to be a restructure of job roles, positions, titles, and compensation structure. The Vice President assures that it will be a good situation for almost everyone involved and that some positions will be upgraded, but a few of the positions may need to be reduced or eliminated. More information will be shared tomorrow as we begin visiting with each of you one by one. We expect to have all discussions completed by the end of this week.

SHAUN'S REALITY

What did Shaun hear? Everyone is going to be fired! No, that is not what was said. But Shaun is very concerned that it could be him that will be one of the positions to be let go. And this is a perfectly normal situation for anyone to be concerned. Organizational restructures are major changes. But with the information given, as we are only human, sometimes our minds can get the best of us, and we tend to focus on the negative aspects of the change only.

Here is a perfect example of where one could stop and critically reflect and think through the SCARED SO WHAT model. We don't need to stop and take the quiz, just think it through in our heads for a few moments of internal dialogue with the best person to listen… ourselves! Follow through the internal discussion with Shaun:

What's going to happen to me?! Am I **Surprised**? Yes, this is scary stuff.

Am I **Conflicted** about this or do I **Champion** this? Well, I'm not sure. They said that some people could get promoted or their jobs upgraded. And for some others they might have their jobs removed. I don't know what to feel. I'm stuck right now, and this is making me nervous.

What **Actions** could I do right now? I don't know what to do... Maybe I could ask some of my colleagues if they have heard anything. Maybe I could go to my director and ask my position in all of this change. I do know Barbara in HR, maybe she will be able to tell me something.

Am I **Receptive** or **Rejective** about this change? Right now, I'm bordering rejective. I like things the way they are.

Have I **Explored** any other options or opportunities? Let's stop for a minute and think this through... I've been exceeding my sales targets every month. Why do I need to be worried? Maybe I'm one who will be ok... Maybe I'm one that might get promoted. Why do I have to think negatively about this? I don't.

Have I made an informed **Decision**? Not yet, I'm a little in **Indecision**... but I'm leaning more towards favorable. I want to do something first to be certain.

These types of change situations are very difficult to process. It is a shame when a company drops information like this and is not prepared to immediately tell everyone what the status or result is for everyone. But this is often a reality within the corporate world. Shaun has started to reflect to himself using the SCARED process of critically reflecting on his situation. And during this, there are already some elements of a strategy coming to fruition. Let's continue the internal dialogue onto the SO WHAT portion.

What is my **Strategy** to get through this? Well, I can go to Barbara in HR and I can also go to my director. I think going to my director as my immediate supervisor is the right thing to do and the first person I should start with. Going to Barbara in HR might bring a conflict of interest on her part and that would be unethical for her and for me. Right now, my strategy is to focus on my good results and be positive and talk with my director first.

Are there any other **Options** or opportunities right now? Not really. They have provided the direction and I need to let it play out.

Do I have a **Way forward**? Yes. First, I'm going to my boss. And second, I'm going to remain positive on my good performance. And lastly, if it is me that gets let go, I am very employable. I'm going to choose to remain positive.

Do I have **Hope** or know **How** I'm going to get through this? Yes, I've got a plan and I feel hopeful. What **Actions** will I take to ensure I'm successful? Remain ethical and talk with my boss. That should provide me an indication and direction.

And how will I **Take ownership**? Setting the meeting with him right now on the calendar for first thing tomorrow.

SCARED SO WHAT is a flexible methodology complete with the SCARED quiz and SO WHAT template to support you in building up your skillsets in managing personal change. In this second scenario, Shaun very well could have stressed on this and built up frustration and unnecessary anxiety and worry. He also could have gone against his ethics and gone directly to his friend in human resources and potentially put her and himself in a conflict of interest situation. When we assume, we are prone to panic and reaction without reflection. This fear and lack of critical reflection can get the best of us and bring out the worst in us. Shaun chose to reflect on his personal change situation and made an ethical plan to speak directly with his supervisor. In this instance, I'm happy to share that while the names were changed, the salesperson was indeed promoted. His hard work was rewarded. But even still, he had the propensity to make an assumption that could have been unfavorable for him. So, the next question that I often get from sales leaders is this: can you use SCARED SO WHAT as a coaching mechanism to help develop sales members through change by focusing on their needs and concerns? Let us look at that now and find out the answer.

What did the research say, and can you
coach with SCARED SO WHAT?

This is an excellent question and I've often been asked this by sales leaders and from other business leaders and academics from around the globe. But before I share the answer to that, I want to share with you a deeper look at my main research questions and findings to prove out whether SCARED SO WHAT would be beneficial or not. As I've shared with everyone earlier in this book, my master's program in leading sales transformation with Consalia Sales Business School and Middlesex University of London is where SCARED SO WHAT was created, researched, and released. My task was to learn how to lead sales members through change and transform into a new way of selling supported with modern sales science and psychology.

My aims and objectives in creating the new personal change model SCARED SO WHAT, were to challenge my own perspectives and bias of the model to discover if it would be simple, helpful, and useful in navigating personal change for my sales members across the globe. In that, I would like to share with you the key findings to the aims and objectives I set out to achieve in this research.

What were my aims and objectives for the research?

1 Package the model into a user-friendly digestible presentation.
2 Engage my employee base in reviewing, ascertaining usefulness and gaining feedback.
3 Introduce externally to my travel agent customer base located in Europe, Middle East, and Africa for usefulness and feedback.
4 Get the model published in a professional journal to share on a broader level.
5 Assess feasibility and usefulness of the model as a mechanism to support the individual's own navigation of personal change.

My first aim and objective was achieved by creating the model on an open public website at www.scaredsowhat.com free for all to use and consume. The second aim and objective was achieved through both qualitative interviews and quantitative survey data measures. The model was also delivered to internal sales members across the globe through a course called "Selling Beyond Covid-19" (Van Ulbrich, 2020a) and had a reach of over 170 employees. The third aim and objective was achieved by creating a new online sales training course within my organization for our external business customers and the general public to consume. A snapshot of that internal research data showed that 1,148 business customers actively engaged in consuming the course that includes the SCARED SO WHAT™ model.

My fourth aim and objective was to get the model published in a professional journal. I was very fortunate that the Chief Editor of the *International Journal of Sales Transformation* was very receptive of the research. As such, it was published the May 2020 edition (Van Ulbrich, 2020b) of the journal for the global sales community to review. Another welcome addition and perhaps a nod that I was truly going into the right direction came when *The Change Management Review* (Van Ulbrich, 2020c) and the Institute of Sales Professionals decided to publish and present SCARED SO WHAT as a model for managing personal change. My fifth and final aim and objective was to assess the feasibility and usefulness of the model as a mechanism to support the individual's own navigation of personal change. In this next section, I will share the outcomes of these research findings.

Research recommendations

It is important for me to recognize that as the creator of this new personal change model, there may be criticism by others in the sales, business and change management communities. I welcome the criticism and conversational dialogue. That is why I am placing this into this book to further the conversation. During my research, I realized and recognized my own bias towards the effectiveness of the new personal change model. That said, I suggested and hoped that the research on the model would continue and that others may construct their own opinions. I very much welcome other contributions and, much like Dr. Elisabeth Kübler-Ross, I only want to facilitate a discussion and I believe this model can do just that.

The data that I have researched during my master's program allowed me to make the following recommendations knowing that they can only be strengthened with further research and collection of opinions.

Simplicity: The new personal change model SCARED SO WHAT presents as a simple tool to use for salespeople aged 26 years and upwards, after careful absorption in following the model as represented on the website at www.scaredsowhat.com. Sales participants interviewed and surveyed found the tool easy, simple, and digestible in understanding its meaning and purpose in both English and Spanish as well as other languages in sampling from around the globe.

Post master's research update: Since my research was conducted in 2018 to 2021, I have received so much support and feedback that the age recommendation has come down considerably. I have had global business customers and even sales employees stating that they are using the model within their family settings and that their children as young as 11 years of age are grasping the concepts of using SCARED SO WHAT as a mechanism for learning how to manage personal change.

Helpfulness: The new personal change model SCARED SO WHAT lends itself as a tool that is helpful for individual use in navigating personal or professional change regardless of if positive, negative, or neutral. It must be noted that the term 'helpful' means helpful in an individualistic way. Helpfulness is in of itself to be determined individually. The model can be used either together or separately, but almost all participants recommend it is more helpful when used together. The consensus is that SCARED helps in navigating feelings towards a change scenario, while the SO WHAT portion helps in developing individual action plans to enact, execute, or deal with a change scenario.

Usable: My evidence suggests that the new personal change model SCARED SO WHAT has presented itself to be a usable tool in navigating personal or professional change. How one chooses to use the model is based on individual needs, understanding of the change being imposed on or with them. However, each participant strongly favors using both the SCARED and the SO WHAT portions together to achieve maximum usability. Respondent 1014 summed up most responses with: "It's important to know you don't have to be scared to use this model. You can use for whatever type of situation you are in regardless of positive, neutral, or negative and no matter if it's personal or work related." And respondent 1001 said this important note that was shared by most: "If you try to do the SO WHAT on its own, you're not dealing with the emotional aspects of change."

Post master's research update: These same findings on Simplicity, Helpfulness, and Usability are only strengthened with continual use from members not only within my sales teams and customer base, but within my organization, to external global corporations, universities teaching with an emphasis on sales and beyond. And now it is being delivered right here to you for your own observations and usage.

A tool for coaching: While it was not my intent to create a tool for coaching, the overwhelming response by the participants both during my master's research and beyond continue to suggest that the personal change model SCARED SO WHAT has the potential to be used as a tool in coaching others. This unexpected observation first came up during my research interview process through respondent's feedback. As a result, I also asked this same question within my online surveys as well to further my research into this aspect. Overall, 88 percent of the survey population with just over 1,100 participants provided a favorable response towards using SCARED SO WHAT as a coaching tool. Another 7 percent had neutrality towards using it as a coaching tool.

Since taking this feedback from the master's program, I have continued to expand using SCARED SO WHAT within my organization. I have created personal change management courses and even secured using SCARED SO WHAT as a coaching tool for sales leaders across the globe within my organization and continue to share it externally. The concept of using SCARED SO WHAT as a coaching mechanism is rather simple. And for a sales leader regardless of if you use this model or another model such as the GROW (Goal, Reality, Opportunity, Way forward) model for coaching, the key element is to realize and recognize that your sales team members have the right to reject change completely. For the most part, the organizational change models we have talked about do not share that as an end result. Rather the opposite—they share that they will accept change. As sales leadership or any organizational leader, you should want to know who your change adaptors are and also who your change detractors or saboteurs might be. If you are delivering and making changes within your organization and teams, you definitely want to ask who is onboard with the changes you are making. For those that are onboard with you, great! Make them change champions. For those that are not onboard with you, give them your support and attention to help them through the change process.

Just like an individual can use SCARED SO WHAT for themselves, as a sales leader and their coach, you can follow the coaching principles by asking open-ended questions utilizing each letter and its representation within the model. For example: "Jayne, are you surprised with the change situation that has happened?" And then wait for Jayne's response. Once you have uncovered her level of surprise you can then move onward. "Jayne, tell me if you champion or are conflicted by this change." And then wait for Jayne's input. And repeat for each letter. "Jayne, what actions have to be taken to understand this change?" None... "Ok, what actions do you think you can take?" And wait for her response.

Continue onward asking open-ended questions until you can help Jayne think out loud and get to a decision point. Remember, at no point should you stop and begin to give your advice, because that would be imposing your own bias and opinions. If you feel you are stuck and need to let the advice monster out, then simply say it: "Jayne, do you want me to coach you on this or would you like my advice?" There has to be a distinct differentiation between coaching and advice giving. Regardless of the decision Jayne has made, at least it would be an informed one. And as her supervisor, you are using coaching as a mechanism to help Jayne through the emotional aspect of change using SCARED as your coaching tool.

The exact same process should be championed when Jayne is ready. She may need to stop and reflect on the change before she makes a decision about it. But when she is ready, if you and she are in a position to continue the coaching conversation, then do so to help Jayne come up with her own SO WHAT plan to action or process the change.

For example: "Ok, Jayne, now that you've made an informed decision, your own decision, can you begin to reflect on what your strategy might be to manage this change? What options or opportunities might you have?" And have that coaching discussion until she has created a beginning strategy. Again, refrain from giving your own bias and advice. The development opportunity occurs when you ask the open-ended questions and Jayne has to think through her own answers. If she comes up with something that may be questionable or potentially harmful, continue coaching by asking questions such as, "What do you think the outcomes would be if you chose that?" or "What do you anticipate the results could be?" The idea is to keep her thinking and reflecting. What is happening during the coaching process is an exchange of ownership and creativity. If you tell Jayne what to do... it's your directive. If it does not work, then she can blame you. But if Jayne comes up with the idea, the strategy plan, and is reflecting on her own needs, then she has full ownership. Why? Because she created it herself through your coaching.

Once the coaching session is completed, only then should you give any further feedback that you feel necessary. But try to make sure that it is supportive and guiding to what is right for Jayne and with Jayne's affirmation. In the final chapter, I will share how I have used SCARED SO WHAT not only within my practice but also in my everyday life. I will also share what is coming next with SCARED SO WHAT and how you can be involved and interact with it through the digital world. I will show you how you can have SCARED SO WHAT all for yourself to use right now and where to get it.

Conclusion

A wider use?

I designed SCARED SO WHAT as a tool to help my sales team members navigate personal change for themselves at work. It was a direct result of my master's program in learning how to lead sales transformation. For a transformation to occur, sales members need to navigate through change and change the way they work from the old ways of the 1980s' consultative sales tips, tricks, and techniques in how to manipulate and force a sale, into the new ways customers want to be engaged and sold to through digital, print, in person, or virtually by focusing on the customers' wants and needs. This means adopting new skillsets and behaviors to embrace positive sales mindsets and focus in on becoming truly authentic while working in a client-centric manner versus the typical supplier-centric methodology we do in global corporations today. If you want to learn more about the basis of this sales science, its psychology, and where the sales mindsets originate, you would be very wise to read the book by Dr. Phillip Squire (2020) called *Selling Transformed: Develop the sales values which deliver competitive advantage* published by Kogan Page.

That said, throughout my experience in creating the model and using it across the globe for my sales employees and B2B customers, I have discovered that SCARED SO WHAT potentially has a much wider use case and feasibility in helping others to learn how to manage personal change for themselves. As I have shared earlier, countless travel agents have commented how the use of the model has helped them to stop and reflect on the changes they were going through during the pandemic. But they in turn have begun to share it with their family members and children, and have commented how easy it is for children from age 11 and upward to digest and understand how to use the model themselves. In these cases, the parents were acting as coaches and asking them how they felt in the SCARED process, such as: "Are you surprised by xxx? Are you conflicted or do you champion the change?" In some instances they had to help them with what the words conflicted and champion meant, but this was a learning opportunity. They would move through the model teaching their children to think and reflect on personal change for themselves. And they could then help them to create their own SO WHAT plan. For me, that is astounding as I had never thought about the wider implications of using the model within family settings.

But what about leaders outside of sales? Could the model be helpful for them as well? In a discussion with a longtime colleague, former supervisor, and friend, I would gain a glimpse to answer this very question. Shannon McKee was one of my first executive supervisors within the cruise industry and has become a lifelong friend and confidante. She transitioned out of working directly for major cruise lines as an executive and formulated her own corporation in leading global cruise line consultancy and partnerships, and is the President and CEO of Access Cruise Inc. in Miami, Florida and has built several companies under that umbrella. I shared SCARED SO WHAT with Shannon early in the pandemic during a dinner conversation I had with her after it was safe to go out again. In our discussion she shared with me how she is normally a champion of change and, as an entrepreneur, she relishes change as an opportunity—especially with building something new like with her companies. Except, normally it is on her own terms.

In her own words:

On March 13, 2020, my world came crashing down. I worked in the cruise industry and the cruise ships came to a sudden and screeching halt. So did my businesses. All of them! I had built three businesses around the cruise industry. It was scary... really scary! I spent my weeks poring over the financials and forecasting the cash flow wondering how long I could keep the companies alive and making payroll. I applied for loans and the Payroll Protection Program. I could keep the company running for at least 6 months with no revenue. But then 6 months turned into a year and so it went on.

Here was a seasoned executive running her own companies and she too was not devoid of the effects of personal change. She has employees to lead and pay and customers around the world that depend on her support and services. She was not exempt from the effects of personal change just by being a chief executive. We continued the discussion, and what she shared with me next led me to believe that the model indeed has a wider usability.

She continued:

> What I realized over the last 18 months is that I was being pushed to change and grow. Using the SCARED SO WHAT model has really helped me understand my feelings and the process. More importantly it has given me a valuable tool for planning. During the Exploration phase, I discovered that I was languishing in a business that was built to fit my lifestyle 10 years ago. I had continued down the path because it was easy, and I felt a responsibility to my employees. Deep down my soul was yearning to begin something new! So, I worked through the SCARED portion of the change model and made a decision. It's time to CREATE again and SO WHAT can help me do that.

And I can share that she has done that. As a seasoned cruise and hospitality industry executive, Shannon kept her businesses afloat and continued to create useful opportunities to support and service the industry and their customers. I'm so very happy to say that coming out of the pandemic her businesses and operations are still going strong. But she's not the only one that I have these types of discussions with. I was able to continue the expansion of the model within the Sales Educators Academy annual conference in 2021. There, I presented among 20+ other academic presenters on the topic of sales education within today's global university setting. My presentation was how to coach sales members through change using the model. And I was so very honored for the model to make it to the top final three considerations for the 2021 annual Sales Educators Academy idea awards (Van Ulbrich, 2021).

I was also able to introduce it with an elementary school principal within my home state. Greg Croomes supervises teachers and functions as the head principal within the Wichita, Kansas public school sector. He invited me to share SCARED SO WHAT with him and his teachers to learn how to navigate their own way through constant changes they are interacting with not only through the pandemic but in daily routines of delivering education to students. It is through conversations, interviews, and discussions like these and countless others, that I am certain that the model has more relevancy and usability than I had originally intended. While it has served me and countless others well in its mission to help people learn to navigate personal change, as each day goes by, I am finding more and more use cases of people not only in sales but from all walks of life who are able to use it for themselves.

The flight continues and we're flying into a trap...

Landing at Miami airport on that sunny and hot afternoon in July 2020, right in the middle of the global Covid pandemic, one would think that I would be in a complete panic situation. Having just let go of so many employees, closed up the sales office in Spain, and packed up my home to relocate back to Miami, I was directly in the middle of massive personal change. I certainly was in a panic after taking off from Barcelona. It was the sudden realization of how final everything was for not only myself but for my family as well. But what happened during that flight would ultimately decide my fate within my role and what would eventually come next for me and my spouse as well.

We spent the first hour on that flight going through the SCARED model together and critically evaluating where we were with the revelation that we were heading towards Miami and America. The reason this was so shocking to me was the fact that, in the United

States, there is no job continuation or job protection process like there is within European countries. Unlike in many European countries, if you are fired or laid off from your work in America, you might not receive anything from your employer at all. All 50 US states are "at will" employment states, which means you can leave your job any time you wish. But, likewise, the employer can let people go any time they wish with or without formal cause. There are exceptions to this but in general you can leave, and the employer can ask you to leave, at a moment's notice. There is an unemployment insurance program in the United States. However, from my own personal experience in surviving a skiing accident in 2000 that made me incapable of working for almost one year while recovering from multiple surgeries, this insurance is nothing that I could depend upon to sustain my earnings and maintain my existing way of life and living. Often it provides far less financial support and results in a significant impact to one's way of living and surviving. And therein was the subject of my surprise, shock, and panic at returning to Florida and being called back to our main work headquarters. I was outright SCARED of losing everything.

As the plane inched mile by mile closer to Miami, we went over each element within the model and talked it out together sitting on that airplane. With a scrap piece of paper, I jotted down each letter and word to ensure that I was critically reflecting on what SCARED meant and could reveal. My husband would ask me, "OK, so you're surprised? How so?" and I would talk it through with him. The act of talking it through out loud facilitated a venting process to help alleviate the stress so that I could think in a calmer way rather than in a panic situation. He moved onto Conflicted or Champion and asked my feelings. And of course, I was conflicted. "How so?" he asked. Together we talked through the conflicting situation at hand. What I had also realized was that he too was conflicted of the situation as it not only was my issue but would ultimately affect his way of life as well. I found this ironic as it is often the case within our sales teams. Something that affects one person, can often affect many.

Then he moved onto asking, "What actions can we take to find a solution?" And that is where we started to uncover some ideas of

how we could make our possible pitch or approach to my organization to maintain and keep my role going even through the pandemic.
From there, I started to feel hopeful and like I had some possibilities,
whereas before I only saw negativity and the fact that as a majority
of employees had lost their jobs, the same fate must also be in store
for me. What I realized then was that I was doing what most people
do today who do not know how to manage personal change. I was
assuming the worst and assuming I didn't have any control over the
situation or outcome. And that is where many people, I included,
typically succumb to the outcomes from change. Was I receptive or
rejective? Believe it or not, I was feeling more receptive from the
possibilities that I uncovered by talking out possible actions. Sure, at
first, I was in a state of full-out rejection. But talking it through, I was
able to transition to a different feeling. And that is the whole purpose
of the model: to understand and give importance to your own feelings so that you can open the opportunity to critically reflect on what
is happening as a result of personal change.

What other aspects of the situation I could explore was the next
question. Finally, am I able to make an informed decision about how
I will react, accept, or combat this change? The answer for me was
yes. I chose to make this dreadful situation a positive one for as much
that I could control. I chose to find a way for me to convey the value
I could contribute to my sales organization and the greater company
goals. But how, one might ask? We spent the next five hours of the
flight looking over the possible options and scenarios of how I could
stay relevant to the organization that was completely shutting down
to protect itself. It is great that I had made an informed decision
about how I felt regarding the change. But the next words out of my
husband's mouth were, "So what are we going to do about it?" We
started out by using SO WHAT to formulate the strategy. We did this
by drawing out a grid on a piece of paper and sectioning off each
element with Strategy, Options, Way Forward, Hope/How, Actions,
and Taking Ownership. And from there, we started to ponder questions of what it was that I could do. Back in Europe, my team and my
supervisor support structure were dramatically reduced to a bare
bones skeletal crew. I was flying back to Miami with no job protec-

tion nor salary continuation but facing the strong possibility of having to apply for unemployment insurance, knowing that whatever that provided would not cover near the expenses we had to maintain our existing livelihood.

Strategy and Options were where the focus of my time was spent. It was there that through talking it out with my partner I discovered how I could convey the importance of keeping the sales teams together, focused, strengthening their own development, supporting their customers, and doing so with continued sales education that supported our travel customers' needs. I was going to report to a brand-new supervisor in the Miami headquarters and he did not know what it was that I was doing nor what my role was for the UK and European teams. This down time would be a benefit to reset the educational support and foundation of our sales teams. My current area of responsibility was for the UK and Europe, but in my Strategy and Options, I laid out how my program was scalable to all international markets to include Asia, the Middle East, the Baltics, India, and Indonesia, as well as down to Australia and New Zealand back up to the South America and Latin American regions.

That SO WHAT discussion focused on the possibilities and the scope of what could be within my role in transitioning back to the Miami headquarters. By the sixth hour into the flight, I had already gone through the shocking realization that I could lose my job as soon as we made it to Miami. From that horrific feeling of helplessness, I had moved on to making an informed decision about the situation and crafted a plan to offer why keeping me would be the smartest option and opportunity for the company during this once-in-a-lifetime situation. My idea focused on this question: when do you ever get a chance to "reset" an entire global sales team without distraction or hesitation? Hardly ever was the answer. Our sales team had literally nothing to sell. No one was going on vacations or holidays and our ships were completely shut down for the unseeable future. Having the components of my plan allowed me to continue on with the process of self-discovery and critical reflection. So, the next question was, do I have a way forward? Feeling hopeful and turning the situation completely around, I answered that question with a sense of confidence. The answer was yes, I feel confident that I have a way forward. But the next question was the tough one. My husband asked me, "Do you have hope or know how it will work?" For that, I paused and had to reflect on it for a bit. Plus, I was distracted because the flight attendant was coming and asked if we wanted beverages or something to eat. One can always use a refreshing beverage.

For me, what the question was really asking was, "Do I believe in myself and my plan?" And the answer for me was yes. Yes, I do believe in my abilities and my capabilities in that I know I can provide a service for our global sales teams that will put them in a better position to sell and support our customers. Not only during this time of need but also when coming out of the pandemic and in our return to service. Yes, I have Hope that this will work, and I know How I need to sell this to my new supervisor. So, the next thing to focus on was what actions I would take once we land in Miami. And for that, I pulled out action items I needed to take in how I would present this idea to my supervisor. That meant that I needed to create a conversation to present the discussion in familiarizing him with what it is that I can offer to help him grow the sales teams, not only right now but in the near future and how the tools and systems and programs that I had built for the UK and European markets could be turned on immediately to help benefit his entire organization. And I was in the best position to help him right size and re-organize his entire operation to a new global standard for sales within the industry. The opportunity was there and the item that I was selling was *me*.

The last part of the model was taking ownership, and for that I simply put together timeline, tasks, and completion items that would be necessary between landing and meeting with my new supervisor. This may seem minor, but it was crucial to have an action plan and timeline of when and how I would hold myself accountable. My goal was to protect and maintain our quality of life and source of income, but to also continue sharing within my organization and career pathway leading sales. The alternative of not achieving this goal and SO WHAT plan was not pretty. No one likes to stand in the unemployment line. I had three more hours on that flight to reflect over my SO WHAT plan. While perhaps I should have, I did not fall asleep. There was too much racing through my mind.

So, what happened?

We landed on a Friday and made our way to our temporary apartment provided by the company. Our house that we had kept in Miami was rented out while we were overseas, and we could not go there. I remember feeling so trapped and kept vacillating back into the SCARED process. Even though I had made a decision and had a well thought out SO WHAT plan, it's still personal change, and until the final meeting with my supervisor had occurred, second-guessing myself and my plan was an active part of my change scenario. I had to remind myself to focus on my plan as that was part of taking ownership. We managed to get settled and unpacked over the weekend. But the conversation to be had with my supervisor was top of the discussion points for the weekend in between unpacking. Opening our luggage and settling in was a good distraction from the looming Monday morning meeting with my new supervisor where I was certain I was going to receive the news of my impending layoff. If that happened, how long could we stay in the temporary apartment? Where will we go? My head was filled with doubts and uncertainty even though I had a plan to share that if my supervisor would only agree to, would certainly provide for our safety and security. Monday morning came and I set up my laptop in the living room to prepare for my virtual session with my new supervisor. We were in the thick of the pandemic and the headquarter's offices were closed. Everyone was working from home. With coffee in hand, I logged into the meeting to meet my new boss. Even with a smile on his face and a soothing voice, I just knew what words were going to come out of his mouth and that they were going to mean trouble.

He was polite and courteous and asked all kinds of questions about the journey and the new temporary apartment. He then started to ask about the teams and how it was to close down the office in Barcelona. He knew it was hard and that my journey in closing out the office, and letting all those people go, had taken a toll on me. I appreciated his kindness and felt that we were making a good connection. I had known him from many years ago. We had worked together in one of our cruise brands when we were both managers. I remembered he was very well liked and treated people with kindness and care. He had done very well for himself and managed to climb the corporate ranks at an early age all the way to Senior Vice President. I remember thinking to myself that I was right. You must treat everyone with kindness and respect because you never know in the future who might be your boss. And this certainly was the case in this instance. But the great thing about him was that, while he had aged a bit and was ripe with experience, his empathy and care for others remained and he was very welcoming. I still felt even though we had made a positive connection, he had bad news to tell me. Maybe his approach and friendly tone would make it hurt less? I almost wanted to just tell him… "Tell me the bad news."

He then changed the questioning to the status of my house in north Miami and inquired if we would be able to move back there soon. And that's when I knew for sure it was coming. The next line he gave me confirmed it. "Well, you know the situation we are in. We haven't been sailing for over five months and we're not earning any revenue. The company is in protection mode," he said. And just then I felt my stomach cringe. Here it comes, I told myself. "Grant, I'll give it to you straight. The most I can give you is six months. You're going to need to secure your own place to live within two months. If you want to find another job, you can, and we won't hold you back. But without any revenues for the foreseeable future, there's no way I can see to keep you onboard," he said. I remember feeling sorry for him. I knew how hard these discussions were because I had just experienced it myself with all of our European teams being laid off and made redundant. He gave me time to reflect and collect myself and his face was almost that of a big brother telling you bad news. I felt that if he could reach through the laptop and give me a hug, he would have done it. And that is when I decided I had nothing to lose, and it was time to put my plan into action.

"What if this is an opportunity for regrowth and level setting the entire international sales organization?" I asked him. I don't think he was prepared for that response, but his gaze went curious, and he said, "How so?" And that is when I completely forgot that he had just given me my notice that I was going to be let go and went into full-on opportunity sales mode. My SO WHAT plan called for the full reset of the remaining international sales teams. A once-in-a-lifetime opportunity while other cruise brands were laying off all their sales forces, for us to be fully investing in our own. I shared with him the role that I had played over the past few years and the sales academy that I had built based off sales science and psychology, and the fact that we could deploy it across all international areas immediately. I then showed him how I would help to organize the full sales optimization process where we could perform job levelling and reset everyone at the same time. This would allow us to align the international team to create succession planning through developmental awareness, skillset, and competency development and be the only cruise brand to invest in our teams and B2B customers in a true time of crisis. The conversation went on and he embraced the discovery of my SO WHAT plan. The outcome was for me to see how much I could get up and running even while we were working remotely. The facts of what he had delivered to me hadn't changed. I still had to find another place to live within two months and get out of the temporary housing. Our home was rented already and under a contract and our tenants were wonderful, so going back home wasn't an option. The six months' job continuation was still there as well. But my supervisor liked the discussion and my plan as it would truly set us apart from our competition and give us the advantage when the time was right to come out of the pandemic and get our ships back into service. He gave me the green light to act but it had to make a significant impact, or the six-month deadline would be enacted. I had work to do. Work to save my job and build for my organization and prove my worth in a job market that had completely crashed. But it was an opportunity that, had I not chosen to embrace the change, would not have happened.

Change is constant

Losing my job in this moment of the pandemic was not an option for me if I had any say in it. My SO WHAT plan had caught the attention of my immediate supervisor. He liked the fact that, in what was seen as a time of crisis, there was an opportunity to crunch down and re-develop our entire international sales force and prepare us to be stronger for our partners and customers when the time was right. The task ahead of me was bold and daring. I needed to take my sales academy, tools, processes, coaching, and support mechanisms that I had deployed in Europe and now take them around the globe in rapid fashion if I was going to make a difference. And, I had to do it all virtually from the new apartment that we had just moved into. Being out of the temporary apartment allowed us the opportunity to settle in for a spell and relax the tension of uncertainty in where we would be living. It also allowed me to ground myself and not focus on the remaining four months I had left until I was to be given my final check. But how to begin when so many others were in the same situation worldwide?

My first focus was to help the international sales team to embrace the same learnings I had just gone through myself. The good thing was that in testing out my new personal change model within my internal organization, the remaining sales team already had working knowledge of what SCARED SO WHAT was. My task was to further embed it to help others get past their own fears in this situation and come up with an individual personal SO WHAT plan for them and their families as well as one for work and how we can progress together. For this to occur, I created a new training module that I could launch within our internal learning management system (LMS) and track the usage with our internal sales team members. Once they had gone through this and learnt even more how to use SCARED SO WHAT, I then used the model as my own coaching tool with our sales leadership and encouraged them to use it with their direct sales reports. People were outright scared of the situation they were in. And as a sales leader, we could not discount the importance and relevance of their feelings. Getting everyone onboard to recognize and critically reflect through their personal and individual situations using SCARED allowed people to embrace what was happening to them. It also allowed for joint conversations between team members. "Have you made a decision?" became the relevant question. For those remaining after the mass layoff, deciding to stay and support our B2B customers was that affirmative decision. We as leaders needed to know if our team members were onboard or not. And while the vast majority of organizational change models suggest that everyone will find their way to acceptance, I wanted to respect each individual's right to choose for themselves. Some people choose not to participate with the change imposed and they eventually leave. Why let that talent go if we don't have to? I wanted to know which one of the sales team members had made a negative decision so that we could possibly help them find a positive decision. For this to work, everyone had to be on the same page together and give their full support. We didn't want change detractors to be sitting out there on their own and causing doubt with their fellow team members. Everyone needed to be doing their part to help his or her customer base through this time of closure and non-revenue generation as well as helping themselves.

The discussions about change were constant as people's individual situations were dramatically changing due to the pandemic. The message was to stay home and work from there but be sure to partic-ipate in the new training programs and continue the dialogue together. Let's take care of each other and grow stronger together. Learning and investing in yourself while sharing your new knowledge of how to sell within an emocracy within the positive sales mindsets will help us to be there for our customers. At that moment, we were not actively selling for the current year. More and more we were simply being there on the other end of the phone to help our B2B customers get through the situation together with us. At that time, we began to share SCARED SO WHAT with our travel customers as they too were hurting and going through significant change. This became a part of our own SO WHAT plan of action. Investing in ourselves and developing our own skillsets while investing in our B2B customers to help them navigate through the process as well.

By the time my six months had come to an end, SCARED SO WHAT was fully enacted throughout the international sales team members as well as with thousands of travel agents we worked with as our B2B customers. I had travel agents from all over our markets telling me stories of how they were using SCARED SO WHAT for teams and their own families. An unexpected delight was that children were using it with parents to help get them through their own personal change situations in dealing with mass quarantines, mask mandates, vaccine acceptance, and the harsh realities of being now home schooled. The sales team across the globe had undergone their new journey of personal learning and development within our sales academy based on sales science and psychology and the specific methodologies in how they should perform in their roles. Travel agents were beginning to find their way in working from home and starting to book reservations for guests for the following year.

Internally, we had just started to lay out the plans for a full international sales team re-organization. This was a beautiful opportunity to align job descriptions, functions, and aspects across the sales career pathway and bring continuity of sales structure and compensation plans to light. And it was also time for me to have that meeting with my supervisor about my departure. My six months had come. It went by so quickly and I felt that I had so much more to do. But the fact was that we were still not sailing. All 62 ships in our fleet were either in cold layup, tied up together side-by-side or floating somewhere around the globe with skeleton crews still onboard. We were starting to sell again for the next year's sailing season and there was a glimmer of hope for a return to service. Vaccines were being produced worldwide and we saw a bright light for a time where we would be sailing once again with paying customers. And yet, I was still preparing myself for the news that maybe it wasn't enough and that I had to go.

By this time, my supervisor and I had formulated a strong connection. Working diligently together to ramp up the skillsets and competencies and support all our team members through embracing personal change was quite the task. We met again virtually and this time the discussion would take a different turn. I was prepared for it and then it came. "With all that you have done to invest in the international sales teams, I'm happy to say that we want you to remain onboard. You've got a lot to do to continue the sales optimization and reorganization and we need you to stay and lead us through that. And we want you to keep growing the sales team. Your job restriction is lifted, and your role is secure," he said. All I could do was to smile and say thank you. He continued to say, "SCARED SO WHAT really works. You came to me, and my task was to notify you your role would dissolve, but you didn't accept that and just take it. Instead, you had a plan not only for yourself, but for our company. And that is why you are staying. It worked and it has worked out very well for all of us." That moment reminded me of an old television commercial for hair club for men. The founder of the hair regrowth club for men said of his formula, "I'm not just the founder, I'm a customer as well." And that resonated with me. I didn't just create SCARED SO WHAT for others to use in managing their own personal change. I used and continue to use the model for myself even today.

By the time of publishing this book, almost three years will have passed since we landed in Miami from Barcelona, and I put my SO WHAT plan into action. It was the first time I had tested SCARED SO WHAT on myself and with my husband. I could not be more thankful for creating this model. One might say that I would have found my way through it and continued onward. But I would argue, why am I any different than the millions of other people that lost their jobs during the pandemic? I'm not any more special or deserving than they are or were at the time. So many others had families that depended on them, and their job was their lifeline and support to keeping everyone else in their care above water. But I whole heartedly agree that by taking SCARED SO WHAT for myself and with my spouse, we were able to stop and critically reflect during a scary change situation. Where in times gone past, I might have made assumptions or knee-jerk reactions and impulses, having the model readily accessible and within my skillset and comprehension to use allowed me to get through that change situation and stop the scary part of change and put together an action plan towards my own success. And I owe thanks to the model and to my professors who challenged me to create it for I am still here and still growing.

As I progressed onward in my personal life and work, not a day has gone by that I haven't relied on the model to help me think through personal change or to coach others through their own situation in personal change. Moving onward into the advance doctoral program with Middlesex University and focusing on sales transformation from a deeper level was something I could have never dreamed of involving myself within. But once I had completed the master's program, I thought, "Why not?" SCARED helped me to think it through, and SO WHAT helped me to continue to engage all the way through it. I would take the model with me daily as I progressed in managing the global sales teams through transformation and transition out of the pandemic each day. And at night and on the weekends, I kept it front and center while doing the doctoral program. There were so many instances where I wanted to give up. But reflecting on SCARED to ask myself how I felt during these times allowed me to make an informed decision to keep going. Sticking to my SO WHAT plan ensured that I would make it through. I'm proud to say, I did.

What do I want for you?

My initial goal was to set out within the master's program and learn how to manage sales transformation within my organization. What I got from that was so much more. If I focused on what the key mechanism was to facilitate transformation, it would be to answer the question, "How do I manage personal change?" And for that, the existing change models did not include the personal element or ability to accept or reject change and then help identify what could be done about it. I had to create something that could be useful and helpful. And in doing so, SCARED SO WHAT was born. Within sales, no matter if you are a sales executive leading other sales staff, a middle manager, or a line employee out on the front lines or on the phone, each of you experience rapid change on a daily basis.

Sometimes it comes in the shape of increased targets, achieving KPIs, creating new offers and making deals, to cold calling and receiving countless rejections. Sales is a challenging yet rewarding profession that takes endurance, positivity, self-assurance, and the capability to constantly challenge yourself to go on further. Add in your personal life, a global pandemic, a global recession or whatever major geo-political event might be happening, along with the demanding needs of your supervisor and you have a recipe for constant change.

Regardless of if you are in sales or in another profession, learning how to stop, critically reflect, and think by using SCARED SO WHAT can help you navigate and manage personal change. For too many years we have been left to get through instances of personal change on our own. We've been led by corporate models and expected to automatically accept the changes imposed upon us and many times without even asking how we feel about the change itself.

What I want for you to take away is this: no matter if you are in a leadership position or an individual on your own, take charge of your own personal change situations. Regardless of if they are happy or sad, make you excited or mad, put yourself in control over change today. To be able to do that, I give you the world's first personal change model designed with you at the center in your ability to accept or reject change. Don't be afraid of change or just make reactions or assumptions. Embrace the change you are experiencing and stop and think it through for yourself. For some of you, the SCARED quiz will be useful. Take it for yourself or take it and share it with a friend and have a conversation. For others, getting to develop your own SO WHAT will be critically important for you in navigating your change success. Use the template as a way of creating your own SO WHAT strategic plan for yourself, today.

And remember: change is constant, it's personal. How you manage it makes it bearable and achievable.

Transforming Sales Management includes learning how to lead others and yourself through personal change to facilitate a "transformation". SCARED SO WHAT is a model that can help you do that. And it is my gift to you. How can you use it?

Where can I learn more and get access to the model?

For individuals

SCARED SO WHAT is available in a few ways. The first way is to go to the main website at www.scaredsowhat.com. There, you will find information about the model along with videos from me sharing how you can use it for yourself. You will also find information about the SCARED Quiz and the SO WHAT template. The model is 100 percent free to individuals who want to access and learn.

The other way to gain access is through the app that you can find for both Apple and Android systems through the app stores on

FIGURE 10.1 The app

FIGURE 10.2 The app business

your mobile phone or tablet. The app will allow you to access SCARED SO WHAT and take the SCARED quiz and build your own SO WHAT strategy and share when set up as a personal account. The personal app for individual use is downloadable today (Figure 10.1).

For businesses and organizations

Businesses and organizations are able to access SCARED SO WHAT on the website as well (Figure 10.2). However, we do have a wider range of options and opportunities to access, teach, and embed this into your employee health and wellness and change management and

FIGURE 10.3 QR code for The SCARED SO WHAT APP

leadership strategies. The SCARED SO WHAT app is downloadable and usable for personal or through a customized business entry point. The business entry point has customizable data subsets, enhanced user ability and reporting that allows a user to share with their supervisor or others within the organization. It can also be incorporated into your existing Human Capital working systems should you desire.

SCARED SO WHAT can be a valuable part of your employee enablement, health, and wellbeing program as well as a key mechanism in your change management and change transformation process for business continuity and change success. Knowing how your employees feel about change and garnering employee and leadership support ensures your corporate change plans are achieved in the way you intend. For speaking engagements, consultancy, app personalization, and company use, please reach out by emailing us at info@scaredsowhat.com.

Further information is available at www.scaredsowhat.com. Figure 10.3 is a QR code which can be scanned to take you direct to the APP.

THE SCARED QUIZ

APPENDIX 1 The SCARED quiz

Name: Jayne Simpson
Date: 5/1/23

Instructions:

Step 1. Think of a "CHANGE" situation that either has happened to you in the past, or is happening to you now. How do you feel about that change? With those feelings fresh in your mind, move on to step 2.

Step 2. Please answer the following 30 questions as honestly as possible. The quiz should take less than 10 minutes to complete. When answering a question you must provide a numeric value for each statement on a scale of 0–7, where 0 = 'never true' and 7 = 'always true'.

		Score
Example	I was excited to hear about the change.	5

My SCARED Quiz Results: WHERE AM I IN THIS CHANGE PROCESS?

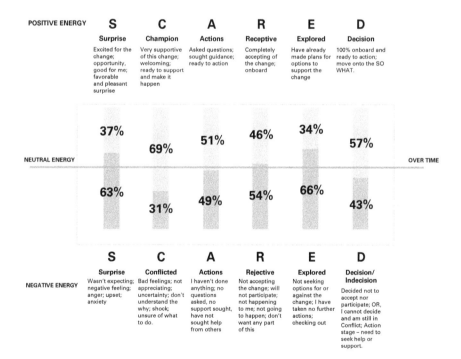

POSITIVE ENERGY

S	C	A	R	E	D
Surprise	**Champion**	**Actions**	**Receptive**	**Explored**	**Decision**
Excited for the change; opportunity; good for me; favorable and pleasant surprise	Very supportive of this change; welcoming; ready to support and make it happen	Asked questions; sought guidance; ready to action	Completely accepting of the change; onboard	Have already made plans for options to support the change	100% onboard and ready to action; move onto the SO WHAT.

NEUTRAL ENERGY ———————————————————————————————— **OVER TIME**

37% 69% 51% 46% 34% 57%

63% 31% 49% 54% 66% 43%

S	C	A	R	E	D
Surprise	**Conflicted**	**Actions**	**Rejective**	**Explored**	**Decision/ Indecision**
Wasn't expecting; negative feeling; anger; upset; anxiety	Bad feelings; not appreciating; uncertainty; don't understand the why; shock; unsure of what to do.	I haven't done anything; no questions asked, no support sought, have not sought help from others	Not accepting the change; will not participate; not happening to me; not going to happen; don't want any part of this	Not seeking options for or against the change; I have taken no further actions; checking out	Decided not to accept nor participate; OR, I cannot decide and am still in Conflict; Action stage – need to seek help or support.

NEGATIVE ENERGY

WHAT DO MY SCORES MEAN: **Jayne Simpson**

The graph above gives you a snapshot of what you are feeling as a result of any possible actions you may have experienced. If you have a lot of dark gray in ACTION, that means you can possibly take more actions by asking questions, sending emails, asking for help and guidance in order to possibly help affect your decision-making. If you have a lot of dark gray in EXPLORE options or opportunities, again, by taking more actions you can impact your overall opportunities that may be available to you.

If you have a lot of dark gray in DECISION, that means one of two things. A) You've chosen to reject the change altogether. You can possibly change this if you want to by taking more actions and/or seeking to explore further opportunities. And if you do not want to and have decided to reject the change....now move onto SO WHAT will you do about it. Or B) you might be stuck in INDECISION, meaning you don't know what to do. Again, by taking more actions like asking questions, seeking advice, phone calls, discussions, reading, etc. you can possibly bring in more information to you so that you can explore further options and hopefully come to a favorable decision.

If you have a lot of light gray in the areas, that is indicative of a favorable action or positive energy. Dark gray is indicative of negative energy.

SOURCE Author

REFERENCES

Introduction

Cespedes, FV and Lee, Y (2017) Your sales training is probably lackluster. Here's how to fix it, *Harvard Business Review*, June 12. https://hbr.org/2017/06/your-sales-training-is-probably-lackluster-heres-how-to-fix-it#:~:text=than%20they...-,U.S.%20companies%20spend%20over%20%2470%20billion%20annually%20on%20training%2C%20and,of%20sales%20training%20is%20disappointing (archived at https://perma.cc/74PU-EZEA)

Consalia (2019) Module 4: Leading Collaborative Change (WBS 4909), Consalia, Hampton Hill, Middlesex, UK, pp. 15, 20–23, 29–30, 36–47,60–88

Cummings, S, Bridgman, T, and Brown, K (2015) Unfreezing change as three steps: Rethinking Kurt Lewin's legacy for change management, *Human Relations*, 69 (1), 33–60

Gartner (2022) Sales transformation strategies: The future of sales, Gartner. www.gartner.com/en/sales/trends/future-of-sales (archived at https://perma.cc/RW83-9FQ3)

Keeling, D, Cox, D, and de Ruyter, K (2020) Deliberate learning as a strategic mechanism in enabling channel partner sales performance, *Industrial Marketing Management*, 90, 113–123

Kornferry.com (2022) Accelerate sales transformation, Korn Ferry. www.kornferry.com/insights/featured-topics/sales-transformation (archived at https://perma.cc/Z33G-A2UY)

Locke, EA, Sirota, D, and Wolfson, AD (1976) An experimental case study of the successes and failures of job enrichment in a government agency, *Journal of Applied Psychology*, 61 (6), 701–711. https://doi.org/10.1037/0021-9010.61.6.701 (archived at https://perma.cc/3GMZ-98GM)

Sarayreh, B, Khudair, H, and Barakat, E (2013) Comparative study: The Kurt Lewin of change management, *International Journal of Computer and Information Technology*, 2 (4)

Tan, CC (2006) The theory and practice of change management, *Asian Business & Management*, 5 (1), 153–155

Chapter 1

Channon, D and Caldart, A (2015) The McKinsey 7S Model, *Wiley Encyclopedia of Management*, pp. 1–2. www.academia.edu/download/60288568/McKinsey_7S_model20190814-24867-1nc2oau.pdf (archived at https://perma.cc/XFC6-P69T)

Creasey, T (2022) The Prosci ADKAR Model: Prosci Tim Talks (online video), YouTube, August 16. https://youtu.be/L_7I03LOyyk (archived at https://perma.cc/FCA4-ARQV)

Galli, JB (2018) Change management models: A comparative analysis and concerns, *IEEE Engineering Management Review*, 46 (3), 124–132

Hiatt, J (2006. *ADKAR*, Prosci Learning Center, Loveland, CO

Hiatt, J (2021) The Prosci ADKAR Model: why it works, Prosci.com. www.prosci.com/resources/articles/why-the-adkar-model-works (archived at https://perma.cc/RY8M-9FJR)

Householder, A (1939) (Lewin, Kurt. Principles of Topological Psychology. Translated by Fritz and Grace Heider. New York: McGraw-Hill, 1936. Pp. 231.), *The Pedagogical Seminary and Journal of Genetic Psychology*, 54 (1), 249–259

Karambelkar, M and Bhattacharya, S (2017) Onboarding is a change: Applying change management model ADKAR to onboarding, *Human Resource Management International Digest*, 25 (7), 5–8.

Kotter, J (2012) *Leading Change, with a new preface by the author*, Harvard Business Review Press, Boston, MA, p. 73

Kotter, J (2014) *XLR8*, Harvard Business Review Press, Boston, MA, pp. 27–34

Kotter, J (2021) John Kotter, Wikipedia. https://en.wikipedia.org/wiki/John_Kotter (archived at https://perma.cc/D9XH-C2UV)

Lewin, K (2021) Kurt Lewin, Wikipedia. https://en.wikipedia.org/wiki/Kurt_Lewin (archived at https://perma.cc/QB3D-CZZL)

Sarayreh, B, Khudair, H, and Barakat, E (2013) Comparative study: The Kurt Lewin of change management, *International Journal of Computer and Information Technology*, 2 (4)

Warrilow, S (2009) Kurt Lewin's Change Model: How to manage change – freeze–unfreeze–freeze, Strategies For Managing Change. www.strategies-for-managing-change.com/kurt-lewin.html (archived at https://perma.cc/U656-35JM)

Chapter 2

Conner, D (1993) *Managing at the Speed of Change: How resilient managers succeed and prosper where others fail*, Villard Books, Random House, New York, NY

Conner, D (2022) Daryl Conner, LinkedIn. www.linkedin.com/in/darylconner/ (archived at https://perma.cc/3LYD-WHQF)

Kübler-Ross, E and Byock, I (2011) *On Death & Dying*, Scribner, New York

Rogel, C. (2010) The SARA model: Learning from 360-degree feedback, DecisionWise. https://decision-wise.com/resources/articles/the-sara-model-learning-from-360-degree-feedback/ (archived at https://perma.cc/6D88-7MML)

Ross, K and Rothweiler, B (2022) Elisabeth Kübler-Ross biography, EKR/Elisabeth Kübler-Ross Foundation. www.ekrfoundation.org/elisabeth-kubler-ross/biography/ (archived at https://perma.cc/299U-YGDR)

Chapter 3

Azamfieri, L (2016) Knowledge is power, *Journal of Critical Care Medicine*, May 9

Bellis, M (2017) The inventors of the first hobby and home computers, ThoughtCo, December 23. www.thoughtco.com/first-historical-hobby-and-home-computers-4079036 (archived at https://perma.cc/37W7-B6XZ)

Birkinshaw, J (2014) The changing sources of competitive advantage, London Business School (online video), YouTube, August 29, https://youtu.be/GVP0tb6FzCs (archived at https://perma.cc/7PZL-Y3VP)

Bouchrika, I (2022) 68 training industry statistics: 2021/2022 data, trends & predictions, Research.com, October 13. https://research.com/careers/training-industry-statistics#:~:text=In%202019%2C%20the%20total%20spending,in%202019%20was%20169.4%20billion (archived at https://perma.cc/3VD3-S55V)

Corrigan, H (2022) Facebook has lost $500 billion since rebranding to Meta, pcgamer, February 23. www.pcgamer.com/facebook-has-lost-dollar500-billion-since-rebranding-to-meta/ (archived at https://perma.cc/7872-TQPH)

Covid19.who.int (2022) WHO Coronavirus (COVID-19) Dashboard, World Health Organization. https://covid19.who.int/ (archived at https://perma.cc/G33D-Z87L)

Dorling, S (n.d.) Top 20 inventions of the 19th century. The Popular List. https://thepopularlist.com/inventions-of-the-19th-century/ (archived at https://perma.cc/LSQ6-EZUP)

Geyser, W (2022) 20 of Instagram's highest paid stars in 2022, Influencer Marketing Hub, August 4. https://influencermarketinghub.com/instagram-highest-paid/ (archived at https://perma.cc/2TFB-D6JB)

Goldstein, M, Martinez, PG, Papineni, S, and Wimpey, J (2020) The global state of small business during Covid-19: Gender inequalities [blog], World Bank Blogs, September 8. https://blogs.worldbank.org/developmenttalk/global-state-small-business-during-covid-19-gender-inequalities (archived at https://perma.cc/M42J-BDTL)

Hoff, M (2022) It's no longer about the virus – remote workers simply don't want to return to the office, World Economic Forum. February 22. www.weforum.org/agenda/2022/02/its-no-longer-about-the-virus-remote-workers-simply-dont-want-to-return-to-the-office/ (archived at https://perma.cc/AT7P-L8AT)

Kirwan, D (2022) Council post: Are social media influencers worth the investment?, Forbes, August 21. www.forbes.com/sites/forbesagencycouncil/2018/08/21/are-social-media-influencers-worth-the-investment/?sh=60ac83f4f452 (archived at https://perma.cc/UW2S-AUHY)

KPMG (2020) Business implications: Covid 19 impacts on global cruise industry [blog], KPMG, March. https://home.kpmg/ae/en/home/insights/2020/03/the-business-implications-of-coronavirus.html (archived at https://perma.cc/KF7M-BQKF)

Kresic, M (2022) Council post: Five reasons soft skills are crucial to successful negotiation, Forbes, February 23. www.forbes.com/sites/forbesbusinessdevelopmentcouncil/2022/02/23/five-reasons-soft-skills-are-crucial-to-successful-negotiation/?sh=d9a3011b1697 (archived at https://perma.cc/VEQ7-3XJG)

Mancilla, A (2022) Top 15 highest-paid Instagram influencers [blog], Blog. hollywoodbranded.com, August 26. https://blog.hollywoodbranded.com/top-15-highest-paid-instagram-influencers (archived at https://perma.cc/G677-SP6M)

Nix, N and Wagner, K (2022) Zuckerberg tells staff to focus on video products as Meta's stock plunges, Bloomberg.com, February 3. www.bloomberg.com/news/articles/2022-02-03/zuckerberg-tells-staff-to-focus-on-video-as-meta-plunges (archived at https://perma.cc/6FC3-FY7B)

Spiegleman, I (2022) Stoli is rebranding to get Russia out of its vodka, Los Angeles Magazine, March 7. www.lamag.com/citythinkblog/stoli-is-rebranding-to-get-russia-out-of-its-vodka/ (archived at https://perma.cc/75VE-5RCF)

Squire, P (2021) *Selling Transformed*, Kogan Page, Kogan Page

Thompson, A (2022) According to geologists, we're living in a new age, Popular Mechanics, January 31. www.popularmechanics.com/science/environment/a22354823/according-to-geologists-were-living-in-a-new-age/ (archived at https://perma.cc/4YKT-2X73)

Web Foundation (2019) As the internet turns 50, we must protect it as a force for good, World Wide Web Foundation, October 29. https://webfoundation.org/2019/10/as-the-internet-turns-50-we-must-protect-it-as-a-force-for-good/ (archived at https://perma.cc/QFY7-G72V)

Chapter 4

Balogun, J and Hope Hailey, V (2004) *Exploring Strategic Change*, 2nd ed., Financial Times Prentice Hall, Harlow

Bassot, B (2016) *The Reflective Journal*, 2nd ed., Palgrave, London, pp. 40–41

Brown, K, Hyer, N, and Ettenson, R (2013) The question every project team should answer, *MIT Sloan Management Review*, 55 (1), 49–57

Consalia (2019) Module 4: Leading Collaborative Change (WBS 4909), Hampton Hill, Middlesex, UK: Consalia, pp. 15, 20–23, 29–30, 36–47, 60–88

Creasy, T (2018) *An Introduction Guide to Change Management*, Prosci.com. www.prosci.com/ (archived at https://perma.cc/VRJ9-RAJP)

Galli, BJ (2018) Change management models: A comparative analysis and concerns, *IEEE Engineering Management Review*, 46 (3), 124–132

Graban, M and Swartz, J (2013) Kurt Lewin: People support what they create, SlideShare, February 21. www.slideshare.net/mgraban/quotes-from-healthcare-kaizen-16674513/58-Kurt_Lewin_People_support_what (archived at https://perma.cc/GE4U-JXDY)

Grant, A (2014) *Give and Take*, Phoenix/Orion Books, London, p. 307

Kotter, J (2012) *Leading Change, with a new preface by the author*, Harvard Business Review Press, Boston, MA, p. 73

Mulholland, B (2021) Change management models: 8 proven examples to evolve & thrive, Process Street, September 3. www.process.st/change-management-models/ (archived at https://perma.cc/8DSA-C9J3)

Schech-Storz, M (2013) Organizational change success in project management: A comparative analysis of two models of change (PhD thesis), Capella University: ProQuest Dissertations and Theses, pp. 20–25

Todnem, R (2005) Organisational change management: A critical review, *Journal of Change Management*, 5 (4), 369–380

Van De Ven, AH and Sun, K (2017) Breakdowns in implementing models of organization change, *The Academy of Management Perspectives*, 25 (3), 58–74

Van Ulbrich, G (2020) A personal change management tool for YOU, SCARED SO WHAT, https://scaredsowhat.com/ (archived at https://perma.cc/Y2BH-KVDF)

Chapter 5

Claxton, G (2006) Expanding the capacity to learn: A new end for education? Opening keynote address, British Educational Research Association Annual Conference, September, Warwick University

Van Ulbrich, G (2020a) Igniting a SPARK – embedding a sales academy into an organization, *International Journal of Sales Transformation*, May 26. www.journalofsalestransformation.com/igniting-a-spark/ (archived at https://perma.cc/A9GF-ADXX)

Van Ulbrich, G (2020b) Introducing a new model for personal change: The SCARED-SO WHAT™ Change Model, *Change Management Review*, July 13. www.changemanagementreview.com/introducing-a-new-model-for-personal-change-the-scared-so-what-change-model/ (archived at https://perma.cc/M7R8-FRJS)

Van Ulbrich, G (2020c) A personal change management tool for YOU, SCARED SO WHAT. https://scaredsowhat.com/ (archived at https://perma.cc/C6YB-GEDQ)

Chapter 6

Conner, D (2012) Change is easy when people like it, right? [blog], Change Thinking. https://connerpartners.com/blog-series (archived at https://perma.cc/KQ9W-NSNU)

Holland, J et al. (2021) Cruising through a pandemic: The impact of Covid-19 on intentions to Cruise, *Transportation Research Interdisciplinary Perspectives*, 9, p.100328

Mandriota, M (2022) How to cope with the fear of the unknown, Verywell Mind, July 28. www.verywellmind.com/i-fear-change-how-to-cope-with-the-unknown-5189851 (archived at https://perma.cc/3XLD-9EZM)

Martinez, O (2021) Timeline: 2020–2021 cruise industry shutdown, Cruise Radio. net, September 2. https://cruiseradio.net/timeline-2020-cruise-ship-industry-shutdown/ (archived at https://perma.cc/4ZRK-FG9H)

McLeod, S (2020) 10 defense mechanisms: What are they and how they help us cope, Simply Psychology, April 10, 2019 (updated 2020) www.simplypsychology.org/defense-mechanisms.html (archived at https://perma.cc/3UM9-T9MS)

McNiff, J (2013) *Action Research*, Routledge, London

Van Ulbrich, G (2020a) Selling beyond Covid-19: Managing through change, Rclcares.co.uk. https://rclcares.co.uk/training/M2_ManagingThroughChange/content/index.html#/ (archived at https://perma.cc/4TM9-PV8Z)

Van Ulbrich, G (2020b) The SCARED quiz, SCARED SO WHAT. https://scaredsowhat.com/scared-quiz (archived at https://perma.cc/4ZWM-VFHC)

Chapter 7

Collins, J (2001) *Good to Great: Why some companies make the leap ... and others don't*, Harper Collins, New York

James, W (1890) *The Principles of Psychology*, Vol. I, Henry Holt and Co, Inc., New York

Kouzes, J and Posner, B (2021) *Everyday People, Extraordinary Leadership: How to make a difference regardless of your title, role, or authority*, John Wiley & Sons, Inc., Hoboken, NJ

Krockow, E (2018) How many decisions do we make each day?, *Psychology Today*, September 27. www.psychologytoday.com/us/blog/stretching-theory/201809/how-many-decisions-do-we-make-each-day (archived at https://perma.cc/5HQP-GVHZ)

Lencioni, P (2020) *The Motive: Why so many leaders abdicate their most important responsibilities*, John Wiley & Sons, Inc., Hoboken, NJ

Lucas, J (2022) Equal & opposite reactions: Newton's third law of motion, Live Science, September 26. www.livescience.com/46561-newton-third-law.html (archived at https://perma.cc/G5U3-P3YC)

Maxwell, J (2010) *Everyone Communicates, Few Connect: What the most effective people do differently*, Thomas Nelson, Nashville, TN

Winkler, D (2010) *Contemporary Leadership Theories: Enhancing the understanding of the complexity, subjectivity, and dynamic of leadership* [ebook], Springer-Verlag, Berlin, Heidelberg. http://ndl.ethernet.edu.et/bitstream/123456789/5287/1/3.pdf (archived at https://perma.cc/M3LL-777M)

Wispinski, N, Gallivan, J, and Chapman, C (2020) Models, movements, and minds: Bridging the gap between decision making and action, *Annals of the New York Academy of Sciences*, 1464 (1), 30–51

Chapter 8

Etymonline.com (2020) option (definition), Etymonline.com, January 5. www.etymonline.com/word/option#:~:text=option%20(n.)&text=1600%2C%20%22action%20of%20choosing%3B,which%20is%20of%20uncertain%20origin (archived at https://perma.cc/P9L5-KZTP)

Mintzberg, H (1987) The strategy concept I: Five Ps for strategy, *California Management Review*, 30 (1), 11–24

Chapter 9

Birkinshaw, J (2014) The changing sources of competitive advantage, London Business School (online video), YouTube, August 29. https://youtu.be/GVP0tb6FzCs (archived at https://perma.cc/P3EG-V7F2)

Van Ulbrich, G (2020a) Selling beyond Covid-19: RCL Cares UK & Ireland, Rclcares.co.uk. https://rclcares.co.uk/en/sales-training.html (archived at https://perma.cc/H584-3R7R)

Van Ulbrich, G (2020b) Igniting a SPARK – embedding a sales academy into an organization, *International Journal of Sales Transformation*, May 26. www.journalofsalestransformation.com/igniting-a-spark/ (archived at https://perma.cc/F2QK-7X6J)

Van Ulbrich, G (2020c) Introducing a new model for personal change: The SCARED-SO WHAT™ Change Model, *Change Management Review*, July 13. www.changemanagementreview.com/introducing-a-new-model-for-personal-change-the-scared-so-what-change-model/ (archived at https://perma.cc/4N6A-FAWB)

Conclusion

Squire, P (2020) *Selling Transformed: Develop the sales values which deliver competitive advantage*, Kogan Page, London

Van Ulbrich, G. (2021) Innovations in teaching: The SCARED SO WHAT personal change model, Sales Educators Academy (online video), YouTube, August 23. www.youtube.com/watch?v=do2DN1qaLWI (archived at https://perma.cc/XXM3-D728)

INDEX

Note: Page numbers in *italics* refer to tables or figures